# THE MARKETING &
# BUSINESS
# GROWTH
# PLAYBOOK

## THE ESSENTIAL BLUEPRINT FOR CLARIFYING YOUR MESSAGE, GENERATING MORE PROFITS, & GROWING YOUR SMALL BUSINESS

### DAN LU

THE MARKETING & BUSINESS GROWTH PLAYBOOK
The Essential Blueprint for Clarifying Your Message,
Generating More Profits, & Growing Your Small Business

Printed in the United States of America.

ISBN: 978-1-7367735-0-5 paperback
ISBN: 978-1-7367735-1-2 ebook

Cover Design by Dan Lu
Interior Design by FormattedBooks.com

# TABLE OF CONTENTS

# INTRODUCTION & ACKNOWLEDGEMENTS

Most small businesses operate well *below* their potential. Even large companies are missing out on massive opportunities for growth. It's not because they don't offer great products and services. They lack the knowledge and strategies that keep them from serving more people, making a bigger impact, and growing their revenue.

Many small companies operate on a *poor* foundation, which leads to wasted time, energy, and money on campaigns, tactics, and efforts that don't yield the best results or, in many cases, no results.

Welcome to **The Marketing & Business Growth Playbook**.

Think of this book as your business plan. It's the blueprint for how you'll structure most of what you do as a company. It'll provide you with concepts, ideas, and frameworks to give clarity to your marketing, improve your growth strategies, and increase your revenue and your profits. It's a no-BS approach absent of fluff and fillers.

My name is Dan Lu and I'm a business growth strategist. Much of what you'll find in this book is a compilation from my mentors. Many of whom I've not yet had the privilege to work with directly, but through their publications and content, I'm honored to share with you what they've taught me.

I'd like to acknowledge Frank Kern, Russell Brunson, Donald Miller, Dan Sullivan, and Jay Abraham for the skills, expertise, and content they've shared. Many more have influenced my approach and philosophy with business growth and marketing strategy, but they are the main contributors who made this book possible.

The decisions you make and the strategies you create moving forward will be based on what you discover here. We'll be diving into a variety of concepts and approaching business growth from *multiple* angles.

Whether you're just launching your company or you're already generating 6 or 7-figures in annual revenue, you'll undoubtedly find at least one tip, idea, or strategy that could make a *dramatic* shift in the trajectory of your business and your life.

This book is valuable for solopreneurs, coaches, local businesses, internet entrepreneurs, online businesses, and even Fortune 500 companies can benefit from the content you'll discover here.

There are things that smaller companies do well that larger companies can learn from and vice versa. And the bigger your company is, the bigger the impact seemingly "small" changes can have on your overall bottom line.

But no matter the size of your business or what industry you're in, having a solid *foundation* is important because so much of your efforts and your results are based on it. That includes your advertising campaigns, your social media strategy, your products/services, and even how you operate or make decisions in your company.

Throughout this book, you'll identify your ideal prospect, learn various ways to scaling your business, and develop *numerous* strategies to achieve the results you desire.

Here's a glimpse of just some of the topics that we'll cover:

- Marketing fundamentals you need to know to get the interest of your target market that will make them want to buy
- The 3 fundamental ways to grow a business so you're not just reliant on getting new clients
- Clarifying your marketing messages to hook your clients and get their attention
- How to turn your traditional website into a leads and sales-generating machine

- Using leverage in your business to generate maximum results with minimal effort
- The 5 WHO's to focus on to improve your business strategy and achieve your goals faster
- How to ethically "spy" on your competitors to gain advantage in the marketplace
- The 4-part framework for finding strategic partners to effectively access more leads and increase your market share
- How to generate more profit from your packaging if you sell physical products
- And much more

The success (or failure) of your marketing efforts will result directly from the work you do here. Your website, graphics, sales funnels, content, social media, copywriting, etc., will all be positively affected moving forward. And your conversions, revenue, and income will all benefit.

Here's what this book is NOT: It's not going to give you the latest and greatest social media hacks and tactics that will be obsolete in the next six months. This book is not about operations, building a team, company culture, nor is it about management.

This resource is also not meant to be the all-in-one solution for marketing. Social media platforms are always evolving and ways of attracting leads, converting clients, fulfilling products/services are constantly changing as well.

What you'll find here are *fundamental* strategies and frameworks that are *evergreen*. Meaning they'll be applicable and useful for many years to come—ideally *forever*.

The goal with this playbook is for you to have a well-rounded approach to growing your company from a variety of angles. You'll go through a *systematic* process to build a strong foundation for your marketing and your business strategy so you can effectively scale.

This book is *interactive*. Throughout most chapters, there will be exercises and places for you to brainstorm ideas, write down answers, and take notes. But because this playbook is intensive and in-depth, there are limitations to a physical and even digital version of it.

As a reader of this book, you get a *free* supplemental guide that you can work with as you go through each exercise. It's a fillable PDF where you can write all your ideas and answers. You can also store it on your computer and as your business evolves, you can come back to it and make changes as needed. Besides the guide, you'll also get *bonus* content.

Visit the address below to access the supplemental resources:

**thembgplaybook.com**

Congratulations on taking this crucial step and investing in this book—your business, life, and family will all thank you for it.

Let's get rolling!

# CHAPTER 1

# MARKETING FUNDAMENTALS YOU NEED TO KNOW

Much of this book will be based on marketing. Therefore, I wanted to dedicate the first chapter to it, so you understand the basics and its importance for growing any business.

Marketing can mean different things to different people. But in its simplest definition, marketing is the activities involved in transferring products/services from a seller to a buyer.

Those activities can include networking, advertising, publishing content, speaking, etc. Basically, anything that helps spread the word about your products/services or your company to generate revenue.

It may not be immediate revenue, but in time, your goal with marketing is to produce a financial or monetary return on investment (ROI). But not all investments require money. It could include time, energy, or other resources—whether that's your own or of someone else's.

Marketing is communication. It's what you say, write, or demonstrate so potential buyers know what you do, what you offer, and how you can help them.

Marketing is sending messages through various mediums like TV, radio, social media, email, webpages, newspapers, magazines, etc. to prospects. It's about educating people and getting them to take action.

For marketing, there are two main types to consider. There's branding and there's direct response.

Branding is what most people think of when they think of marketing. It's what you see with major companies like Apple, Nike, Samsung, etc., when you come across their advertisements. Branding is about associating a certain thought or emotion about your company. It's about positioning your business in the marketplace so people perceive you to be the *only* choice when it comes to who to purchase from.

And although branding is valuable and has its benefits, it's *not* the best approach for small businesses and companies.

With direct response marketing, its main objective is getting people to take *immediate* action when they come across your content or advertisements. That action isn't always to buy right away. It could be to visit a website, click a link, submit contact information, call a phone number, etc.

This is a more straightforward and "aggressive" approach, but not in a pushy, sleazy way you might think.

When you have smaller budgets for marketing, it's important that you spend it wisely and that it's *profitable*. When you focus on direct response, you're able to track your results and improve upon them much more easily than you could with traditional branding.

Now, that's not to say you shouldn't focus on branding at all. It's important to consider and implement *both* into your overall marketing strategy but if you had to favor one, focus more of your efforts (and your budget) on direct response marketing.

Throughout the rest of this chapter, we'll dive into several concepts and strategies that are important for every entrepreneur and company to know. These ideas will lay the groundwork for the rest of this book.

## "Customer" vs "Client"

Before we dive into the core of this playbook, I want to make a very important distinction. This is something I learned from world-renowned business strategist, Jay Abraham.

Most businesses operate under a premise that they serve **customers**. And according to Merriam Webster's Dictionary, a customer purchases a *commodity*. Instead, you want to view everyone that purchases your products/services as **clients**.

Clients are defined as **one under the protection of another** and it's usually associated with industries that provide professional services like lawyers, consultants, real estate, and so on.

While the definitions that differentiate the two may seem minimal, the mindset and approach for business and marketing strategy are profound. I'm not saying you should stop using the word "customer" or "consumer". If those are the terms you've been using, then keep using them. This isn't advice on semantics. Instead, it's a shift in how you *think* about the people that buy from you.

When you view everyone that engages with your company as a *client* versus a customer, how you treat them is different. The way you speak and market to them is different. How you serve them is different. And all for the *better*.

Even if you're "just" offering products, you still want to think of your fans, followers, leads, audience, etc., as clients, not customers. So throughout the rest of this book, I will use the term *client*(s) but understand that includes those who would normally be called customers or consumers.

## The Concept of Preeminence

Continuing on with the concept of serving clients no matter what business you're in, the next topic is about preeminence—also popularized by Jay Abraham. In its essence, you want to position yourself and your company as your target market's most *trusted* advisor.

To be a leader in your space, you have to position yourself as the go-to resource for your prospects and clients when they're looking to address their problems, challenges, or goals. Remember that as a client, people and businesses are under *your* protection.

Preeminence is about knowing your client better than they know themselves. It's about providing more value than everyone else—even *before* the exchange of money. It's about servicing clients at the highest level, educating them, and helping them make the best decision(s) for *them*. Preeminence is about putting their needs *above* your own.

When you're preeminent, you're anticipating questions and problems before they arise and you're able to address them clearly for your prospects and clients.

It's about being authentic, helpful, and genuine. This will attract people to your company. This will make them want to do business with you. And this will also make them loyal clients who will market your business for you even *after* you're no longer serving them.

## Client-Based Marketing

One of the biggest mistakes and flaws of most companies, small or large, is basing their marketing and their messaging around themselves and not the very people they serve.

And while that works to a degree, when you focus your marketing around the people you want to attract, your messaging will be more effective, you'll convert more leads, and you'll generate more sales.

The reason most businesses focus their marketing and messaging around themselves is that it's *easier* to do. Most do not take the time to understand who they serve and because of that, they talk about their company and their own story.

Now, there is a time and place to share information about you or your business. However, your *clients* are the foundation of virtually *all* of your marketing efforts. It's the basis for your website, your sales funnels, your advertising campaigns, your email marketing campaigns, and much more.

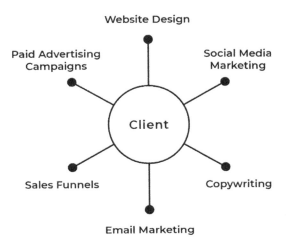

Figure 1.1: Your clients are the center and
foundation of your marketing strategy.

You need to speak to what your *clients* want and as Donald Miller talks about in "Building a StoryBrand", people are generally looking for ways to survive and thrive.

The better your messaging can explain to your prospects how your company or product/service will help them with their survival or how they can thrive in their life, the more likely they'll do business with you.

And that's why much of this book is dedicated to helping you get to know *who* you're serving. When you do, you can create the right messaging that will resonate with them and this will improve your conversions at every level.

## People Buy for Emotional Benefits (Generally)

For the majority of purchasing decisions, understand that people often buy for their own *personal* gain. And for every transaction, there's usually an underlying emotional incentive.

A popular acronym in marketing is WIIFM—What's In It For Me?

And often, we're thinking about how we can survive or thrive as mentioned earlier. But even deeper than that, we're constantly doing things to either avoid pain and/or gain pleasure.

Pain could include stress, fear, worry, embarrassment, jealousy, and other negative emotions while pleasure includes joy, satisfaction, love, prestige, self-worthiness, and so on.

Later in this book, you'll learn how to speak to the pains and pleasures of your target market so you can truly connect with potential clients.

## AIDA

Another popular concept or framework in marketing is AIDA — Attention, Interest, Desire, and Action.

The first step is getting your ideal audience's attention, which could be done through advertising or content marketing. This is why it's so important to have your marketing be *client*-centric (not business-centric) and emotion-based as previously mentioned.

Once you get their attention, the next step is to develop interest. What will you say to get people to want to learn more about what you offer? What can you do to get them to move further along your client journey?

After interest, your goal is to then create desire. That means finding ways to get people to *want* your products/services. Even better, if you can get a person to feel like they *need* what you offer, then it's almost guaranteed that they'll buy from you. To do that, you have to clearly convey the benefits of what you offer and how it will positively affect a client's life.

When you have a person's attention, built interest, and created desire, it's then time to move them to action. It's very important to make it *clear* and *simple* for people to take the next step in your business so they can get the results they're after.

Throughout this playbook, we'll work on developing the strategies to address each part of this framework and cover additional concepts to better your business.

## Client Journey

No matter what business you're in, there's a general cycle or flow through which you want people to move through. It can be broken down into stages and within each stage, you have various strategies and tactics.

Ideally, you want to attract visitors to your business, convert them to leads, build a relationship by providing value, have them become a client, experience great results or benefits, and then refer your business to others to go through the same process.

Figure 1.2: The typical client journey through a business.

Like the previous topic, you'll be guided through each step in more depth throughout the book!

## The Decision See Saw

There are 4 main reasons that people don't buy...

1. They don't want what you offer (you can't really do anything about this)
2. They don't believe that you can deliver the results they're seeking

3. They don't believe in *themselves* to get the results (they may believe that it works for *others* but not for them)

4. The timing may not be right

When someone first sees the offer for your product/service, they enter into their decision-making process. That means they'll weigh the pros and cons, advantages or disadvantages, and benefits or drawbacks.

This process is *unique* to every person. Some make quick decisions while others do extensive research and comparison before making a purchase—small or large. But generally, the more expensive a product/service is, the more information and the more *time* they need to evaluate before making a decision.

I like to explain this concept by comparing it to a see saw. Before a potential client is introduced to your offer, they're *neutral*. They have no thoughts, feelings, or real emotions about it.

Figure 1.3: A person doesn't have any thoughts
or emotions yet about buying.

But once they see your product/service and its cost, perhaps through a sales page or after a sales call, their mind will automatically enter into a mode where they list all the reasons and experience negative emotions that tell them they should *not* make a purchase.

This includes their fears, doubts, worries, insecurities, past experiences, price concerns, skepticism, etc. So, imagine these reasons piling up on one side of the see saw and tipping it to a point where their decision to buy is a *no*.

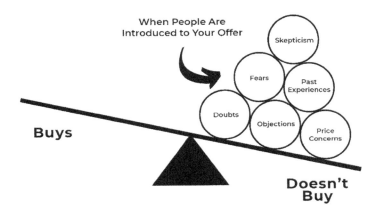

Figure 1.4: After seeing an offer, a person usually develops
a list of reasons not to buy even though they want to.

A large role of your marketing is to counteract all of their reasons with reasons *to* buy—it's about shifting beliefs. And you want to do this in an **ethical** way. You should not be manipulating someone to part with their money if it's not the right fit for *them*.

Again, we want to treat people as clients and therefore, they are under our *protection*. If it's not in their best interest to do business with us, we have to be honest, accept it, and do what's best for *them*. You may "lose" a sale here and there, but overall, you'll operate a much better business with this mentality and approach.

So how do you tip the see saw the other way and get people to buy if it will truly benefit them? It's by providing valuable reasons on why they *should* become a client and doing it in a strategic way. That includes sharing testimonials, case studies, listing benefits, talking about the pain of inaction, and more.

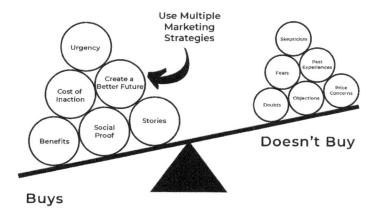

Figure 1.5: Your marketing needs to provide reasons or help them develop their own of why they should buy—those reasons need to "outweigh" reasons for not buying.

And the fourth reason people don't buy is because it just may not be the right timing. It's not because they don't want what you offer. It could be due to their finances, their physical, mental, or emotional state, where they are in their career or life, etc. A 'no' isn't a 'no' forever—it just means not right now. That's why it's important to keep in contact and have a strategic follow-up process.

In the following chapters of this book, you'll develop a list of reasons why people *should* buy from you and you'll learn exactly where you can use that information throughout your marketing.

## Cheaper, Faster, Better

There's this concept that consumers want things that are cheaper, faster, and better. And while that may be true with *certain* products/services or industries, it's not a great general philosophy to build your business by.

Certain demographics are more price-sensitive than others. Certain groups of consumers or clients want things to be faster and faster. And most do want products/services to constantly evolve and get better.

But if all people wanted things cheaper, there'd be no market for luxury, high-end goods or services. If all people wanted things faster, everything would be marketed as "instant". But this is definitely *not* the case. Just look at what you buy in your personal or professional life. Is it the cheapest and/or the quickest? Most likely not.

The main thing you want to focus on are **results**. People don't buy products/services, they buy what those products/services can and will do for them. And it doesn't always mean they need the result(s) immediately and it doesn't mean you have to be better than everyone else.

Besides results, another crucial factor in a company's success is the **relationship** they start, nurture, and maintain with clients.

So even more important than cheaper, faster, better is the *know, like and trust* (KLT) factor. What people care about most is that they can trust your company and that you have *their* best intentions as a priority. Again, it goes back to the philosophy of treating everyone as a *client* and the concept of preeminence.

When you build rapport with people and you earn their trust, they'll view you as the *only* source who can help them achieve the results they want. It's not about being the quickest, it's not about being the absolute best (even though you should always strive to be), and it's not about being the cheapest. And that brings me to my next point…

## Do NOT Base Your Business on Lowest Price

Here are two big mistakes a business can make in their strategy: First, it's trying to *become* the cheapest in the market. And second, it's actually *marketing* their products/services as the cheapest or the lowest cost option.

When your goal is to be the cheapest, you're constantly battling slim margins. They'll get tighter as your business grows which makes it much more difficult to scale sustainably.

Remember, people are *not* always looking for the cheapest, they're looking for value and results. And if you are the cheapest now, understand that someone can and will likely undercut you at some point, which will force your company into a very difficult situation.

Also, most people associate extremely low prices with *poor* quality. They assume if prices are too low, then the products are likely made poorly or the services offered are below average. It's not always true but in most cases, it is. So not only are your margins going to be slim, but you'll also eliminate a large segment of the market who do not want rock bottom prices.

When you talk about how low your prices are, you immediately give potential clients a reason to "price shop". They're now judging and comparing your products/services based on cost and this could ultimately make them choose a competitor over you.

Instead, focus on increasing the *value* of what you offer. That means providing more benefit or more results to your clients. That will allow you to charge higher prices, so you're not constantly fighting for scraps at the bottom of the barrel.

Now, there is an exception to this. If you have a strong *backend* to your business, meaning you have additional products/services you offer and know that most clients make additional purchases, then you can promote the low price of an *introductory* or initial product/service. We'll cover more about the backend of a business later.

But again, your core philosophy should *not* be based on being the lowest in the industry or the cheapest available.


## Your Target Market Matters

Your ideal client has a *huge* impact on your marketing and business strategy. For example, if you're selling to business owners or companies (B2B), you'll have very different messaging and approaches versus if you're selling to "normal" clients or consumers (B2C).

Not only does the *type* of buyer matter but also their income/revenue level. How you market to and structure your business will vary depending on how much your ideal client generates annually and has to spend. What you say to them, what you offer, and how you fulfill your products/services need to match the expectations and requirements for that particular group of people.

If you're selling high-end goods to wealthy, prestigious entrepreneurs who earn $1 million/year, your marketing and business approach will differ greatly than if you're selling to a lower or middle-class person earning $50,000/year. The same is true if you're offering services.

For example, let's say I own a landscaping business. I could target companies with large grounds or plots of land that need to be maintained. I could target wealthy company *owners* with large homes. Or I could target smaller homes in a middle-class neighborhood.

One job for a company might be $5,000 in revenue while a job for a home might be $50-500. You're essentially performing the *same* service (of course, there's more work involved), but your pricing, expenses, and profit margins will be very different depending on who you're serving. This is true for any professional services, whether you're a realtor, an accountant, a lawyer, or a plumber.

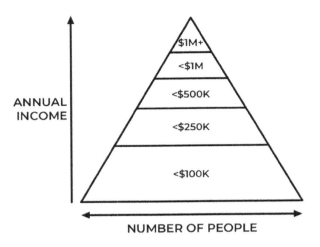

Figure 1.6: The Client Income Triangle.

As a person/business's annual income increases, the number of people in that group *decreases*. Generally, the wealthier a person or company is, the more funds they have available to spend on products/services for their business or their personal lives.

Wealthier people are generally busier, so they are more willing to hire *outside* services. They purchase higher-end products and goods with better profit margins for the businesses they buy from. And they usually have a larger network they can refer to your business.

On the other side, if you target lower-income people or households, they're much more price-sensitive and they generally shop around for better deals. Your pricing will matter much more and you'll likely have thinner profit margins.

If you target wealthier people, you don't need to "convince" as many people to say "yes" to your products/services to achieve the *same* revenue targets.

Now, there is no right or wrong in terms of who you choose to cater your business to and who *you* want to serve. It's totally up to you. But the goal here is to understand the differences between markets and how it impacts your strategy.

With your marketing, your messaging, your visuals, etc., it will vary dramatically depending on *who* you're targeting. Different markets have different buying criteria and they buy for different *reasons*.

In a later chapter, we'll dive more into getting to know your client which will improve your messaging for your target market. But for now, think about who you *truly* want to work with because again, it has a major impact on your strategy and your results!

## It's Not What You Market, It's How You Market it

Marketing is a science and an art at the same time. On the one hand, you need creativity to produce advertisements, find attention-grabbing images, or write engaging copy. On the other hand, there needs to be tried-and-true formulas or frameworks to follow if you want results.

As you likely know, marketing is a huge part of any business and plays a major factor in their success. Maybe you've seen commercials or ads for certain products and thought to yourself, "How is that product successful?!" Whether it was an informercial or an ad on social media, you've probably had that thought cross your mind a few times—if not *many*.

And sometimes, it's in a crowded market where there are dozens of other businesses offering essentially the same thing. So what separates those products/services from others? How do they become the leader in their industry?

It's because they have a better *strategy*. That could mean a better message, better visuals, a better sales process, and so on. But one of the best ways to differentiate yourself leads to my next point…

## Don't Be a Commodity

I talked earlier about viewing people who do business with you as *clients* and not customers. Again, customers are people who purchase a commodity.

And with that same mindset, we want to make sure that you don't have a commodity in the market. We don't want to offer something that is easily comparable to what others are offering, whether that's in features, benefits, or in price.

With such a low barrier to entry to start a business these days, there's more competition than ever. So it's important to ask yourself how you can differentiate or add more value to your offerings to make them stand apart from the crowd. And this leads to the next topic of discussion...

## Unique Selling Proposition

Also known as your USP, this makes you *different*—and preferably better— than your competitors. It's what allows you to stand out in the marketplace.

Your USP can include your pricing structure, how your product/service is the original one of its kind, impeccable client service, your bundling of additional products/services, quick fulfillment process, super-fast delivery speeds, convenient location, a long-term return policy, proprietary technology, outstanding strength or durability, risk reversal strategy, or your guarantee offer.

There are two main goals for having a USP. First, it's to differentiate so what you offer is not easily comparable to others in the market. And second, it's to increase the chance that people make their *first* purchase with you. Depending on your USP, it could also be the reason that clients continue to make purchases time after time.

Often, the first sale is the *hardest* because people are still learning about you and they haven't yet experienced your products/services. But once they do and they have a great experience, then making additional sales with that same client will be much easier.

Therefore, it's extremely important to do what you can—ethically— to get people to *try* your products/services. Ideally, you have one strong USP you can really leverage throughout your marketing. Like in branding, your USP can lead to that one main thought or emotion people associate when they hear about your business.

As an example, if your USP is a 365-day money-back guarantee while everyone else in your market offers a 30-day guarantee, then your offer reduces the "risk" for someone to try your product/service better than anyone else in your industry. This makes you stand out and gives you an advantage.

Another example would be if you bundled products/services in a way that offers greater value to the client. Other companies may offer similar items but do so individually. This makes ordering more complicated and more expensive for potential clients. By bundling, you can give clients better purchasing options and even allow them save money. The idea is that if you can make just *one* part of your offer unique, you will increase your conversions of new clients.

Now, you might think it's tough to create a USP for your company or your products/services. Especially in a world where there seems to be so many other businesses doing or offering something similar to what you do. But that's why you must dig deep and get *creative* in how you develop and share your USP.

And understand what may not seem unique or interesting to you may to a potential client. It might be something that's common knowledge to everyone in your industry, but to an "outsider", it could be what attracts them to you and ultimately makes they buy.

For example, let's say you have a process for how you create a product or fulfill a service. And maybe it's similar to how *most* others in your industry do it. But potential clients likely won't know that. So if you share a story in your marketing about how you use a particular method to make your products or how you help clients get results from your services, that could be the key differentiator that makes you stand out in the market.

Remember, it's not just what you market but *how* you market it.

## Does Design Matter in Marketing?

Now, we'll switch gears a little bit and talk about design. Visuals *do* matter in your business. Therefore, the design of your website, images, videos, graphics, sales pages, etc., make an impact on your results.

Design is about *communication*. It's about expressing and stimulating thoughts, ideas, and emotions. We're visual beings and we make split judgements and decisions based on what we *see*.

Design isn't just about fancy graphics or pictures. It's about layout, colors, structure, spacing, and flow. So if your website, brochures, social media images, or book cover is unattractive, you could be doing more harm to the success of your business than you think.

Have you ever gone to a webpage where everything was poorly spaced, the colors clashed, or the text size/font was so difficult to read that you left right away? Most likely. And that means that the website is missing out on potential leads and revenue for the company.

Design might seem like a small detail in the grand scheme of things for marketing and strategy. But again, we're *visual* beings who base decisions on what we *see*. If you're a small company that wants to grow, you have to consider design in your marketing—don't neglect it.

## Chapter Takeaways

This chapter was really about understanding the *fundamentals* of marketing and to introduce you to various topics to help you while progressing through this book.

I could have gone deeper into each topic, but I wanted to give you enough information to understand the overarching concepts without overloading you. But you now have a solid foundation from which we'll build upon chapter by chapter.

For marketing, here are the key things to remember:

- View everyone you do business with as a *client*, not a customer
- Put your clients' best interests above your own

- Create *client*-centric content and messaging that attracts attention from your target market, create interest and desire, and gets people to take action (AIDA)
- Do not base your business model and/or marketing strategy on lowest price
- Focus on increasing the value of your offers
- Differentiate yourself with a unique selling proposition (USP) so you're not easily comparable to others in your industry
- Who your target market is matters—the type of clients and their revenue/income level has a major influence on your marketing and business strategy
- Do not neglect the impact of design throughout your business and the effect it has on your results

# CHAPTER 2

# WHERE ARE YOU AND WHERE ARE YOU GOING?

Like using a GPS, we need to know where you are and where you're looking to go in your business in order to find the best path. We also want to know any constraints or boundaries you may have. That way, when you learn the different ways to scale your business, you'll know which strategies to implement (or not) to reach your goals.

Now, to grow your business, you need to take an *honest* assessment of where you are right now. Whether you're just getting ready to launch or you're operating a 6 or 7-figure company at the moment, it's important to understand your business as it is today and get clear on your goals for the future, whether that's 1 year, 3 years, or 5+ years from now.

Below, you'll find questions to assess your business. The goal is to get a "snapshot" so you know where you are and you can create a vision for your future.

After reviewing your business, we'll also dive into your current marketing strategies to get an understanding of what you're doing, what's working, and what's not working.

Again, once we know where you are, we'll have a better idea of where we need to make improvements moving forward. If you're just starting your business and you have no data yet, then you can skip to the next section where we dive into your goals.

Eventually, you can come back to this section once you've generated revenue and have numbers to work from. Remember, you want to *constantly* analyze your business so you can find ways to improve it.

This part of the book is by no means a formal evaluation. It's really just to give you a *glimpse* of your business, identify where you are, and discover what assets you have.

To download the free supplemental guide and bonus resources, visit:

**thembgplaybook.com**

*What result(s) does your client get from using or experiencing your products/ services? Think beyond surface level and dive into why people are truly buying your product/service. Is it saving time, making more money, to be happier, healthier, less stressed, more security, etc.?*

_____

_____

_____


*How much do your products/services cost? You could have multiple prices here.*

_____

_____

_____

*What makes you or your products/services unique from your competitors and stand out in the marketplace? Think about your USP.*

_____

_____

_____

*If you don't believe that you're unique, what can you do to set yourself apart from your peers?*

_____

_____

_____

*What is the average lifetime value (LTV) or total revenue per client that comes to your business?*

_____

_____

_____

*How much revenue did your company generate last year? Are you on track to match or exceed that number for this year?*

_____

_____

_____

*What are your best performing products/services that are responsible for the majority of your sales? What are your worst performing products/services?*

_____

_____

_____

*What are the biggest challenges or obstacles that are preventing you from reaching your financial goals? How long have you been stuck or unable to hit your revenue targets?*

_____

_____

_____

## Creating a One-Liner

If you could describe your mission in *one* sentence, what would it be? Think about WHO you serve and WHAT you do for them. Address a PAIN POINT of theirs to get their attention. Also, share your main BENEFIT. Your benefit should be linked to what's important to your *client*.

Here are some examples...

- We help small businesses create tax strategies so they can pay less to the government and increase their profits.
- We help new mothers improve their overall wellness so they can have more energy to take care of and play with their young children.
- I help chiropractors generate 50-100 new, quality patients every single month, so they never run out of business.
- Our computers provide the fastest processor in the market so people can work efficiently and never worry about equipment slowing them down.
- Our team provides homeowners with state-of-the-art security to keep their loved ones safe and out of danger.

*Below, write down your business/company's one-liner statement. Use the 3-part formula as a foundation—you can always refine it later. This one-liner could be used for your pitch, your website, your tagline, business card, in media, on your social media profiles, etc.*

_____

_____

_____

_____

_____

## Marketing Strategy Assessment

Now that we've addressed your business, let's assess your current marketing strategies and your social media platforms.

*Facebook (Page Likes, Followers)*

_____

*Instagram (Followers, Average Comments/Post)*

_____

*YouTube (Subscribers)*

_____

*Twitter (Followers)*

_____

*How many people are on your email list?*

_____

*How many phone numbers do you have for leads and/or clients?*

_____

*How many website visitors are you getting/month?*

_____

*How many Yelp reviews do you have? What is your overall rating?*

_____

*How many Google reviews do you have? What is your overall rating?*

_____

*What is the most successful marketing/advertising campaign you've ever run? List the details, the offer, and the result.*

_____
_____
_____
_____
_____

*What is the worst marketing/advertising campaign you've ever run? List the details, the offer, the result, and the lessons learned.*

_____

_____

_____

_____

_____

*Why have clients bought and continue buying from you? You can get answers from past clients, surveys, your testimonials, or any other means of feedback.*

_____

_____

_____

_____

_____

*Why DON'T people buy your products and services? Price, competition, confused by your marketing, etc.? Learn why people don't buy so you can address them in your products/services or your marketing.*

_____

_____

_____

_____

_____

This was a crucial step. Like a doctor diagnosing a patient through questions and testing to better understand their situation, it's important we do the same for your business. Because a business is almost like a *living* organism. You have to constantly monitor it and make sure that it's healthy at all times.

## Where Are You Going?

Now that you know where you are, let's talk about where you want to go! In this section, the goal isn't to lay out the exact blueprint for how to achieve your goals.

It's for you to have a clear picture of what you want for and from your company. And it's not just about a single revenue number that we're after. We also have to consider what your *life* is like as an entrepreneur or business owner.

It's crucial that you factor in what your day-to-day will look like as part of your planning. If you're operating a successful business but feel like you're not enjoying the process, *now* is the time to get a clear vision for what you want.

Go through each question below to find out what you want your company to look like. Answer *truthfully* about what you want—don't worry about what other people want for you. It's ultimately *your* business which you can design to fit your goals, your needs, and your dreams.

*What is your ideal annual revenue for your business? What is your ideal annual income from your business?*

_____

_____

_____

*How big of a team do you think you need to produce that type of revenue? Are you looking to grow a large company or would you rather stay smaller?*

_____

_____

_____

*What would your daily activities in your business be? What are you great at, passionate about, and enjoy doing?*

_____

_____

_____

_____

_____

*How much time do you want to work in your business? Do you want to work as few hours as possible or are you okay with working 40, 50, 60+ hours per week?*

_____

_____

_____

*Where do you want to operate your business from? Remotely? A downtown office? A commercial building in a quiet neighborhood?*

_____

_____

_____

_____

_____

*Write down any other goals, wants, desires, or visions you have for your business.*

_____

_____

_____

_____

_____

Now that we have a vision for what you want, we can now dive into the frameworks and strategies to help get you there! We quickly envisioned the who, what, when, and where of your business, but take more notes on anything else you can think of that's part of your vision.

Again, I hope you were *honest* with your answers. Remember that you have the ability to design *your* ideal business—no one is forcing you to do anything (at least I hope not).

As it's important to know what you want, it's just as important to know what you *don't* want or what you'd like to avoid in your business. This will give you even more *clarity*.

*Write down everything that you don't want to have in your business.*

_____

_____

_____

_____

_____

The following chapters will provide you with various marketing and business growth strategies so you have *multiple* options to achieve your revenue or income goals. That way, you're not limiting your thinking and therefore, limiting your results!

## Chapter Takeaways

- This chapter was about assessing where you are and where you want to go
- Think about the who, what, when, and where of your business and why you want or don't want those things
- Make sure you're honest with your answers as this will give you clarity and make it easier to strategize from here on out

# CHAPTER 3

# SCALING YOUR COMPANY

When scaling a business, there are many things to consider. As a company expands, their expenses usually increase and typically, at a *faster* rate. And if not planned for in the *initial* stages, those expenses can be much higher than expected, diminish your profit margins, and they could hurt your ability to build cash reserves.

It's hard to know what expenses to consider when you've never been to a certain stage in your business unless you learned from the experiences of others. Depending on your type of business, you may need to consider staffing, team building, infrastructure, company culture, training, health insurance, travel, inventory storage, fulfillment, shipping, customer service, etc.

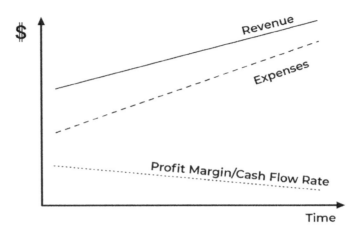

Figure 3.1: As revenue increases, expenses increase at
a faster rate and profit margins generally decrease.

That's why this chapter is so important. It's to give you a variety of
concepts so you can improve existing strategies, brainstorm new ideas,
and scale your business effectively.

For growing a company, there are 3 *fundamentals* ways to do so. Most
people naturally gravitate towards acquiring more clients when they're
looking to expand. While new clients are the lifeblood of any business, it's
only one way and often, it's the *hardest* way.

*Most* businesses want more **revenue**—not necessarily more clients.

Here are the 3 fundamental ways to grow a business:

1. Acquire more clients.
2. Increase the average cart value or revenue/transaction. And there
   are 2 ways to do this:
   a. Increase the price of your products/services.
   b. Sell more products/services in each transaction.
3. Increase the frequency of transactions per client.

These may sound *basic*, but now that you know the 3 main ways to scale, you can expand your thinking for how to grow your revenue. Strategies 2 and 3 are really about increasing the Lifetime Value (LTV) of each client. When looking at LTV, it's important to consider how much people spend with you over the *entire* duration that they're your client.

This means looking at repeat purchases as well as other products/services they buy from you. LTV is a value that most businesses *should* know but do not.

Besides knowing your LTV, another important metric is Allowable Acquisition Cost (AAC). This is what you're able to spend to gain a *new* client. If you advertise, this value lets you know what you can afford to spend and still be profitable with your campaigns.

This differs from Cost of Acquisition (CA), which is how much it *actually* costs to gain a new client for your business versus how much you *can* spend to gain a new client.

LTV is important to consider because you may acquire a new client "at a loss" from their *initial* purchase. But if you have strategies in place for people to buy more, you can afford that "loss" upfront to be profitable later.

Here's an example to give you some clarity…

Let's say you sell a product for $100 and your initial AAC is $15 once you factor in all expenses (i.e., production costs, storage, overhead, fulfillment, etc.) and the profit margin you desire that's associated with that product.

And let's say you have an advertising campaign and each new client costs you $20 to acquire. Initially, you might think to stop the campaign because you're digging into your profit margins for that product. Or, if it exceeds your profit margin, it may seem like you're "losing money" to acquire each new client.

However, if each client on average makes 6 more repeat purchases over their lifetime, that means they spend $700. And this means that your campaign will be eventually be profitable—not initially but over time.

This also means that your AAC is actually much higher once you factor in those repeat sales. Therefore, you have to make sure that you look at the big picture and not just focus on initial sales. Remember, it's about *lifetime* value.

This is how (and why) so many companies have low-priced, *introductory* offers. It's because they know that one of the hardest parts of business is acquiring *new* clients. Therefore, they lower the barrier of entry to get new people "in the door" of their business to become first-time clients.

And once they're in, the company knows that what they offer is valuable and that clients will continue making purchases. This, of course, will increase their LTV. Note that not every single client will buy again but a large enough percentage will to offset and outweigh those that don't.

The more you can increase the lifetime value of each client, the higher your AAC will be which means the more you can spend to gain new clients and still be profitable. If you're advertising, this gives you an advantage over your competitors who may not have a high LTV and therefore, they can't spend as much to advertise their business.

Here's another example: Let's say your product's price is $100 and your expenses for it is $50. That leaves you with an AAC of $50 before you lose money on that sale. And let's say 25% of 100 people convert on that offer to yield $2,500 in upfront revenue. If they make 3 more repeat purchases, the total revenue would be $10,000.

Now, let's say you lower your price to $50 so that for every *initial* sale, you're breaking even or perhaps "losing" some money upfront because of the acquisition cost. But instead of a 25% conversion rate, it's now 50%. That's still $2,500 in *upfront* revenue.

But now you have an *additional* 25 clients you can market your products/services to on the *backend*. Again, let's say each person makes 3 more repeat purchases at the full price of $100. That's a total revenue of $17,500 and a difference of $7,500 in revenue just by changing the *frontend* offer.

The goal of this was to illustrate how lowering the barrier to entry (i.e., changing price) will convert a higher percentage of *first-time* clients and how it impacts the amount of revenue overall because of repeat purchases.

Most businesses and companies are shortsighted and they don't think about a *long-term* relationship with their clients. But if you have a strong backend to your strategy that spans over months and years, that's where you can have tremendous growth and improve your revenue and profits.

Figure 3.2: The first sale for every new client is just part of the overall LTV. It's the backend that makes up the majority of a company's revenue.

Below, we'll dive deeper into various ways of growing your LTV so you have different options for effectively scaling your business.

## Sales Funnels

Although not a brand-new concept, it's one gaining more awareness and rightfully so because of its power to increase the average cart value or revenue/transaction (second way to grow a business)—especially in the *online* marketing space.

The term 'sales funnel' can have different meanings depending on who you're talking to and what industry they're in. For this book, we're specifically talking about funnels designed to offer multiple products/ services in the *same* transaction.

This is not to confuse you with the more general concept of a sales funnel, which explains how a person goes through various stages such as awareness, interest, consideration, evaluation, and purchase.

The power of a sales funnel is the ability to increase the average cart value of *every* transaction that occurs in your business. This can yield massive increases in revenue from seemingly "small" additions or changes to the checkout process.

Sales funnels aren't just for selling products or services online. They can be applied to offline businesses as well.

One of the most popular examples to explain this concept is with McDonald's. The addition of a *simple* statement (and offer) of "Would you like to supersize that?" or "Would you like to add fries to your order?" is their way of increasing the average order value.

It's subtle yet strategic and that additional revenue goes a long way when you're talking about hundreds, thousands, or even millions of transactions. And not just over the course of a year but over the *lifetime* of a business.

The main reason sales funnels are so powerful is because they're based on the concept that people in a buying state are more likely to buy at *that* point in time. Therefore, you want to offer your products/services when they're in the mindset of trying to solve a problem or address a need/desire and ideally, while their payment information is already in the system.

Sure, you can offer additional products/services at a later time, but this will be more challenging as you now have to "convince" people to pull out their credit cards, enter their information, and go through their internal decision-making process once again (remember the see saw explanation in Chapter 1).

If you can strategically combine the purchases into *one* transaction in an ethical way, then that is ideal. And what you offer in your sales funnel has to make sense for the client's original purchase. You do not want to offer additional products/services if it's not related *and* beneficial to the buyer.

For a successful sales funnel, it's important to know your client and what they're trying to accomplish with their initial purchase. From there, you can plan for what other products/services they would need to solve their problems or achieve their goals.

For many people, they don't know what they need. So it's up to *you* as a business to do the research and anticipate for them.

You can get creative and find ways to apply sales funnels to your checkout process, whether you have an online or offline business. They can be very basic with just a couple of steps or they can be quite complex and extensive with multiple steps.

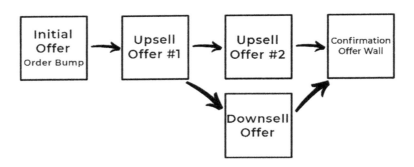

Figure 3.3: An example of an online sales funnel
showing the various offers a client would receive.

Let's say someone is buying a product from your online store. On the checkout page, they get offered an Order Bump where they can add a relevant product/service to their cart with just *one* click. When they click the "Buy Now" button, their order is submitted.

But instead of going straight to a Confirmation Page, they are then offered a complementary product (Upsell #1)—perhaps at a discount. If they say 'Yes', they get taken to another offer (Upsell #2). If they say 'No', they get taken to yet another offer (Downsell).

After they're finished going through the funnel, then they are directed to the Confirmation Page where they're shown listings of additional products/services they might be interested in on what's known as an 'Offer Wall'.

Note that there are *limits* to this. You do not want to offer your potential clients too many upsells. This will likely annoy them and prevent them from doing business with you again.

Now that you have a general concept of sales funnels, let's look at a simple example with some numbers. Let's say you're selling a product that cost $30 to 5,000 consumers/clients through your website.

**Single Product Checkout:** 5,000 x $30 = $150,000 total revenue

**Funnel with 1 Upsell:** Upsell costs $20 and 20% of buyers take it (1,000 people). That means an additional $20,000 in revenue and $170,000 in total revenue.

**Funnel with 2 Upsells:** Upsell #2 costs $25 and 10% of people who bought the first upsell buy it (100 people). This is another $2,500 in revenue for $172,500 in total revenue.

**Funnel with 2 Upsells and 1 Downsell:** Let's say we have a downsell of a $15 product for people who did *not* purchase Upsell #1 (4,000 people) and 20% buy it (800 people). This yields $12,000 and results in $184,500 in total revenue.

Hopefully, you can see how each example builds upon the previous one by adding additional products in the *same* transaction. And if you're selling *physical* products like in this example, combining purchases helps reduce shipping costs. So rather than mailing out multiple packages at separate times, you'd only have to ship everything *once*.

Note that these are arbitrary numbers and it's for example purposes only. It's to show how to increase revenue with additional offers that are *strategically* placed throughout a *single* transaction. Imagine how you could apply this concept to all of your checkout processes and the results it would have in your business.

Let's look at an example with actual items. Say you offer camping equipment and someone is purchasing a tent through your website. When they add the item to their cart and submit their payment, you might make them an offer for a cooler as your first upsell. The next upsell might be a firepit to keep them warm at night and a possible downsell could be a lamp or flashlight.

The client may not have thought about these other items but realized that they actually do want them. Again, it's about anticipating what they might need and then presenting it in the right way at the right *time*. And because they're in the buying state and getting ready for their camping trip, they'll be more likely to buy during that *same* transaction rather than waiting until later.

Now, to further incentivize people to take your upsells or downsells, you can offer a special discount that won't be available at any other time. This creates a sense of urgency and helps people quickly make a buying decision.

I hope that simple example helped you visualize the flow of a strategic sales funnel and the power of offering additional products/services during the *same* transaction. There are a lot of strategies and tactics that go into properly building funnels, but hopefully, you can see how and why they're effective for scaling your revenue.

Again, it helps you increase your average order value. If you have a lot of transactions in your business, increasing the average order size by even a little will compound to create a massive difference in your results over the long-term.

Do sales funnels apply to every single niche or industry? Perhaps not in the same way that I just shared, but you can get creative and incorporate the *principles* of it into many business models.

Now, I want to point out that this strategy is different than what you would see on most retail websites, where they list a few options under the "Customers Also Bought" section on a product page, in the cart, or near the checkout area.

Sales funnels strategically place offers *after* someone has clicked the "Buy Now" or "Place an Order" button—not before. The difference is not just in the timing of when additional products/services are offered but also *how* they are offered (i.e., giving a limited-time discount to incentivize people to make a purchase right then).

Other funnels to consider using for your business are lead funnels, which acquire leads and build your email list (we'll cover this topic in more detail later in the book).

Webinar funnels get prospects to watch an educational video that provides value and tries to convert them to clients afterward. Application funnels get clients to apply to work with you.

There are more types of funnels but those are just a few to show you what's available. To learn about the art and science of funnels, I recommend reading "DotCom Secrets" by Russell Brunson.


## Value Ladders

Let's now dive into value ladders, also known as ascension ladders. You might be familiar with the concept but you may have never taken the time to learn about them or understood how they can be applied to your business.

Value ladders are essentially a suite of products/services that a business offers to their clients based on what their needs are—usually varying in price.

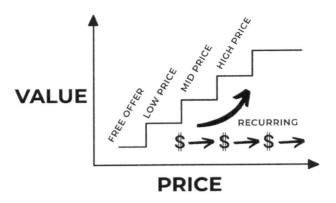

Figure 3.4: An example of a basic value ladder to illustrate different offerings at different price points depending on the need and wants of the client.

Your clients are likely at different stages in their journeys and might require different products/services based on what their challenges and/or goals are at *that* point in time. By offering a variety of options for people at different stages, this increases the chance that a person does *some* form of business with you because your offerings can appeal to a wider range of the market.

Before making larger investments, people usually start at the bottom of a value ladder and *ascend* or work their way up.

At the bottom of the ladder, it's usually something that is free or low cost. This could be an introductory offer or something that is inexpensive to produce and fulfill. At the top of the ladder, it's usually products/services that offer higher value and are the *most* intimate and/or require the most resources—this is why the price is higher. Resources could mean time, energy, money, personnel, etc.

Generally, a brand-new, first-time client will start at the bottom of the ladder. Once they get a specific result and/or you've proven that you can help them with their goals, they'll likely ascend up the ladder and purchase your other offerings.

You can have offers that range in price from free to $1,000+. You can start at $5,000 and go to $100,000+. Many different factors dictate *your* value ladder, including but not limited to your industry, your competition, your client demographics, your ability to market, the value of what you're offering, etc.

Offers at the top of the ladder tend to have the *highest* profit margins. This is because you're offering more valuable services, selling higher priced goods, or because you're strategically bundling products/services together that save money on labor, fulfillment, shipping costs, etc.

A concept to consider for your company is creating a high-end service or program at the top of your value ladder. You can label it as "diamond, platinum, elite, gold, signature, VIP, etc.". You may have seen this strategy with major airlines or car rental companies. The idea is to create an "exclusive" service.

Why does this work? Because people generally want to be a part of a *special* group where they're treated differently than other clients—they're treated *better*. Many people want more attention, extra care, and they want access to perks that others don't have access to.

And guess what? They're willing to pay for it.

Remember, it's *not* about price. It's about results, benefits, experiences, and feelings for the end client. As I mentioned in a previous chapter, *who* you market to matters. Wealthier people will generally invest in higher-end goods and services and they want to be treated to higher standards.

They associate with different types of people, they work and live differently than most, and they enjoy being serviced at a higher level. Therefore, having an upper tier service or program can make a huge difference in your revenue if you package your products/services strategically for your target market.

Now, it doesn't mean you have to actually serve high net-worth clients to have a high-end offer at the top of your value ladder. People in the lower and middle-class also like to feel special and experience higher-levels of service. After all, who doesn't enjoy getting access to special perks, rewards, or incentives?

This concept isn't about servicing the affluent. It's about the innate desire that people generally want to be of a higher status and the desire to be treated with more attention and care. Wouldn't you be interested to learn how to be a part of a businesses' Signature VIP Program and all the perks that come with it?

Remember, it's not just what you market but *how* you market it!

Now, onto some examples. Let's say you have a chiropractor office. Your first offer may be an introductory session for *half* of the regular price. The next offer on your ladder may be a 3-session package, then a 5-session package. Maybe your top-tier offer is your "Gold Package" that includes 10-sessions with a massage in each, which you can't get with any other package. Another way to change your offers is to vary your session *duration* (i.e., 30 minutes instead of 15 minutes).

Now, let's say you sell physical products and let's assume it's something people would typically buy more than once (i.e., supplements, personal care, food items, etc.). Instead of having *different* products at various price points, you can offer different sizes (i.e., 16 oz vs 8 oz). Or you can create bundles, which could reduce shipping and maybe even packaging costs (we'll talk about how to get more from your packaging later in the book).

But note that not everyone has to start at the bottom of your value ladder and work their way up. Some might come into the middle of it or even start at the top and work their way down. Again, it depends on where they are in their journey and what they need at that time to reach their goals.

But get creative here and try different strategies. Again, by offering a variety of options, you'll appeal to a larger percentage of the market with different needs and goals.

Now, understand that a value ladder is *not* required for your business.

You can have just *one* main offer and stick with that. Sharing this topic tries to expand your thinking and give additional ways you can serve your target market and grow your business. It'll come down to *your* goals and what you're looking to achieve—a value ladder might not be necessary or even applicable for your business.

And remember that if and when you do offer other products/services, there are *opportunity costs* to consider. You want to make sure you have the resources—time, energy, money, personnel, infrastructure, etc.—to handle your various offers.

## Recurring Revenue

One of the biggest challenges entrepreneurs and companies face is *predictable* revenue/income.

You have consistent expenses you know you have to pay each month but your number of leads and clients fluctuate. This can cause a lot of concern, uncertainty, and stress for a business.

So, can you *ethically* create a recurring revenue stream? Can you implement a *subscription* model where clients are paying monthly, quarterly, or bi-annually? Instead of one-off, sporadic purchases, how can you *systematically* get clients to return to your business and produce predictable and consistent cash flow?

In many industries, people actually *need* to purchase products/services repeatedly. But they don't do it because they forget or they get sidetracked. Life gets in the way and they don't think to re-purchase items even if they had great results or a great experience.

Think about how clients can stay with you on a consistent and more long-term basis. Can you structure or offer your products/services in a way so your revenue is not starting from *zero* every single month?

This will depend on your industry and what you offer, but if you can create recurring revenue in your business, you'll operate with more *confidence* knowing you have revenue coming in the following months. This allows you to make better decisions, take more chances to grow your business, and give you more peace of mind as an entrepreneur and/or company.

## Upfront Cash vs Recurring Revenue

Now, we just talked about the power of having recurring revenue in your business. That's what many businesses should strive to create so they have a more predictable revenue stream. But let's take that concept to a different level.

Another option to consider is collecting cash *upfront* but still offering your products/services over an extended period. Usually, this offer comes at a *discount* for the client to incentivize them to pay *now* and save money over the long run.

Now, you may be thinking, "Why would I take less money overall but still provide the same value in terms of my products/services?" And that's a great question!

And I'll answer that with another question: Would you rather take cash upfront now and have it in hand or would you rather *maybe* get cash later on?

Here's the thing: There's no way to guarantee that a person will come back to your business. Even if they have a great experience, they might take another offer from a competitor and they may never return. Therefore, having cash upfront can be more important and valuable than waiting to collect it over time. And that brings me to my next point...

Another benefit of collecting cash upfront is that clients may stay with you over a *longer* duration. Someone who commits to pay up front to stay for an extended time (i.e., 1 year) might mean they actually stay with you *longer* than they would if they were on a traditional month-to-month plan.

Also, your incentive for paying upfront doesn't necessarily have to be a discount. You can provide other incentives such as adding products/services to your offer that aren't available anywhere else. Or, instead of discounting the price for a certain amount of time, you can extend the time but keep the original price (i.e., get 2 extra months of service for free if you pay for a full year today).

So what's another benefit of collecting cash upfront?

Well, if you have a "marketing machine" or "money multiplier" that can *predictably* grow your capital, having more cash in hand will allow you to scale up faster.

So it's not about discounting your products/services or "losing money" because you're getting less in dollars—it's about what you can do with the money *now* to improve your business over the long run.

For example, let's say an advertising campaign is producing 5 to 1 return on ad spend (ROAS) and it's very profitable. Ideally, you'd want to put as much money into that marketing machine as possible! Of course, there are limitations and issues with growing *too* fast and your business would have to sustain the growth on the operations and fulfillment end. But again, the concept behind this approach is what you can do with the money today to improve your business over time.

You'll see this upfront-cash-collecting strategy with many software companies. They offer a month-to-month plan, but they also offer a reduced-priced option if you paid for the whole year (or more) upfront.

Now, if you don't have a profitable marketing machine like an advertising campaign, then this is something to look into for creating a *predictable* source of leads and clients for your business.

## Who You Serve Matters

In an earlier chapter, we talked about the concept of who you market to matters. But it's a topic I want to reiterate again in this chapter because it does affect how you scale your business. It's not just what you offer, but *who* you offer it to that can have a profound effect on your company and your revenue.

To quickly recap, if you sell to other businesses and companies (B2B), they're willing to spend and invest the *most* into products and services. If you focus on upper-class or wealthy clients, they have more funds, they're not as price-sensitive, they're more open to outside help, and they typically know more people (who also have high incomes) that they can refer your business to.

If you're a B2B company, who your clients serve and the price points of *their* products/services is also important. Just as there are major differences in B2C markets, the same is true for B2B.

If the companies in your target market sells 5-figure services, it's much easier for you to sell higher-ticket products/services to them as they only need one or a few sales to recoup their investment with you and get a positive ROI.

However, if their average sale is only $20 and you're offering a product/service that costs thousands, it's more difficult to "convince" them to make a purchase because they'd have to generate hundreds of new sales to recoup their investment. This isn't an issue if they're already bringing in a large amount of revenue and have the funds to invest.

Again, the point of this isn't to tell you which market to serve—it's up to you. The goal here is for you to understand that if you're B2B, who your clients serve and what *they* offer (low vs. higher-priced products/services) all have an impact on your business and your results. It's something you should consider when determining your target market.

With wealthier clients (either B2B or B2C), your pricing is generally higher, which can allow for better margins. And to hit certain revenue goals for your business, you wouldn't need to service as many clients as if you were offering similar products/services to a lower or middle-class market.

Remember, people rarely buy based on price—especially the wealthy. They buy based on results, benefits, prestige, status, experience, and emotions. And to get what they want, they're willing to pay more and they have the funds to do so. If you want to charge higher prices, consider serving a more affluent market and/or increase the value of what you offer.

## The Fortune is In the Follow-Up

You may have heard that *the fortune is in the follow-up*. If you've been in business for a while, then you've probably heard it often. But are you actually following up enough? And are you following up in the right way?

That doesn't just mean with prospects you want to convert to clients. But it also means following up *after* they've become your clients. Many people understand the power and importance of following up, but they don't actually do it.

Instead, they're constantly trying to find new leads while not working the ones they already have —even ones they've paid for. This is a major mistake of many small businesses. Even larger companies fail to strategically communicate with their leads and clients.

One of the most powerful forms of follow-up today is still *email*. Yes, there are other options available such as texting, calling, or even messaging bots. But email is still the *top* source for converting leads to clients and generating business.

Even though email inboxes are more cluttered today than ever, it's still a place where people have some of their *most* valuable communications and conversations. Important content from friends and family, financial information, entertainment updates, and more are all in their inbox. That means people still do check it *frequently*.

Think about how many times a day you check your own inbox. I can almost guarantee at least *twice*—maybe even more. Yet, many businesses fail to leverage email to acquire new clients and continue communications for repeat purchases.

Now, another saying you may have heard is that "the money is in the list". But it's not just the *size* of your list that matters. It's also the *relationship* with the people on your list that's important.

One common and big mistake that businesses make is offering *newsletters* on their website to get people onto their mailing list. This is *costing* companies everywhere a lot of money, especially if they get any reasonable amount of traffic to their site.

Here's the thing: Most people's inboxes are already cluttered—they're not looking for a newsletter or more information. What they want are **results**.

So most people won't even consider opting into your mailing list and therefore, they won't even receive your email follow-up sequence. That is unless you have a retargeting pixel that can track your visitors and reach them through other platforms (which I highly recommend you have installed on your website—it's free).

But even still, how long is your follow-up sequence? Are you helping people and providing *value* in your emails? Are you staying top of mind by contacting them frequently enough?

One of the most important aspects of all marketing is the follow-up. And the average number of touchpoints for someone to do business with you today is much *higher* than it was before.

Why? Well, because there's more competition for people to consider and there are so many more distractions that prevent people from acting. That means you have to be much more *strategic* and think *long-term* with your follow-up process.

A big challenge that businesses face with building an email campaign for new leads is coming up with content for what to say. In a later chapter, I'll share ideas and frameworks to build your follow-up sequences for both new leads and new clients.

## Help Your Clients Win

Too many businesses gladly accept money from their clients and once they do, they feel like their part is done—it's very transactional. Instead, you want to focus on helping your clients succeed *after* they've paid you.

Think about where your clients usually fail or veer off course. Think about the common mistakes people make in their journey when trying to achieve the results your product/service is supposed to help them with.

What can you do to help them stay on track? What can you provide to get them results faster? Can you offer another level of service as part of your value ladder?

If you increase your clients' success rate and help more people get the results they desire, the more goodwill you'll build with them and the more likely they'll refer others to you. So as a byproduct of creating more successful clients, your business will grow.

## Rewarding Your Best Clients

Many companies offer special deals or discounts to acquire *first-time* clients but neglect the ones that spend the most, buy the most often, or have been clients for the *longest* time.

Can you create unique programs, offer exclusive bonuses, or give special perks to your most loyal clients that no one else can get? The goal is to make them feel appreciated and valued for being a high-value client. It also helps ensure they'll stay with you no matter what your competition offers.

Remember that people aren't usually buying based on price alone. It's the *relationship* your business has with them that matters more. And one way to improve that relationship is treating your loyal clients with more attention and providing more value so they stay engaged with your company.

An example of this strategy are hotel and credit card programs. If you book a certain number of nights or spend a certain dollar amount within a year, you're put into different tiers or programs that unlock various perks or bonuses. By having certain marks to aim for, this incentivizes clients to use your products or services more often so they can hit those targets.

## Asking Better Questions for Growth

Something I learned from Tony Robbins is that the quality of your life is determined by the quality of the *questions* you ask. That philosophy can be transferred over to business as well and it's something we have to do *consistently*.

If you ask better questions, you'll get better results and conversely, if you ask vague or poor questions, you'll get poor results. So why is this important?

Well, questions will guide your mind and your thoughts. It's something we're doing constantly throughout the day. And if you ask more focused and deep questions, it'll always yield better results in both business and in life.

An example of a poor question would be: "How do I grow my business?" Now, that's vague and broad. If we get more specific, you might ask, "How can I get more clients?" But is it really clients you want or is it more revenue?

The next question would be "How do I increase my revenue or my profits?" Then, we can go even deeper and ask, "How can I increase my profits without spending more money?"

And "How can I increase my profits without spending more money or hiring more employees?"

Now, hopefully, your mind is trying to come up with answers to address these questions. Besides revenue goals, you can ask questions relating to *time*. For example, "How can I work 10 fewer hours per week but still generate the same income?"

Your questions will depend on your specific goals but after going through this chapter, you now have some strategies (i.e., value ladders and sales funnels) to brainstorm ideas for achieving those goals. But we'll get into some more concepts as we go on.

When you add more focus and constraints to your questions, it'll produce clearer, more powerful answers, and therefore, better results. As we move through the rest of this book, I'll be asking a lot of questions so we can get better answers that will improve your marketing and business strategy to help achieve your goals.

Below, brainstorm ideas for the various strategies discussed above.

*How can you create a sales funnel for your business? What additional products/ services can you offer to your clients? Think about your core offer, upsells, and downsells. Again, sales funnels aren't just for online businesses; they can work for offline businesses as well.*

---
---
---
---

_____
_____
_____
_____

_What types of offers can you have in your value ladder? Think about low, mid, and high price. Can you create a "top-tier" offer or program that provides clients with special treatment or access to additional products/services? If so, what will you call it (gold, platinum, elite, diamond, signature, VIP, etc.)?_

_____
_____
_____
_____
_____
_____
_____
_____
_____
_____

_Is there a way for you to generate recurring revenue for your company? Write down ideas for a recurring revenue program(s) you can offer and list ways that it'll benefit your clients._

_____
_____
_____
_____
_____
_____
_____
_____
_____

_____
_____
_____
_____

*Can you create an upfront cash offer(s) in your business? What sort of incentive(s) will you give clients to take your upfront cash offer versus recurring payments? If you collect cash up front, what will you do with it? How will you use it to grow your business?*

_____
_____
_____
_____
_____

*Write ideas of how you can increase your clients' success rates. What can you do or offer to help ensure they achieve the results they're looking for?*

_____
_____
_____
_____
_____

*Write ideas for how you can reward your best clients (i.e., spends the most, been with you the longest, refers the most, etc.). What do they need to qualify and what will you offer them?*

_____
_____
_____
_____

_____

_____

_____

_____

_____

## Chapter Takeaways

- The 3 fundamentals ways to grow a business are to acquire more clients, increase the average transaction value, and increase the frequency of transactions for each client
- Sales funnels increase the average order value by strategically offering more products/services in the same transaction
- Value ladders are a suite of products/services at varying price points that help clients depending on their needs/goals
- A recurring revenue model helps produce predictable income each month
- Collecting cash upfront can fuel your growth faster if you have a revenue-generating vehicle that can effectively multiple your capital
- Who your target market is (and who they serve if you're B2B) affects your pricing, your offers, and your revenue
- Most transactions and sales come from the follow-up process so you must have a powerful strategy for generating leads, converting them into clients, and maintaining relationships for repeat purchases
- Increasing your client success rate will increase the chance that people continue doing business with you and refer you to others
- Rewarding your most loyal clients will make them stay with you longer and continue purchasing your products/services
- Ask more specific, clear questions to get better results in your business and life

# CHAPTER 4

# USING LEVERAGE TO ACHIEVE GOALS FASTER

Now that we've discussed the fundamental ways to grow any business and various strategies for increasing revenue, we'll now focus on a very important and powerful topic that *every* company needs to consider if they want to scale efficiently.

And that is the concept of *leverage*. When a company focuses on using leverage, they'll undoubtedly find more effective ways to address problems or challenges and grow their business. But what does leverage mean? How does one look into leverage for their business?

Leverage means using a quality or advantage to achieve a desired result. In our case, it means utilizing *other* businesses' resources to improve *your* business. It's trying to generate maximum yield with minimal input. And ideally, it's beneficial for *all* parties involved.

If you have a challenge, a problem, an obstacle, a roadblock, etc., that's keeping your business from reaching its goals, there's a good chance that there's some way you can use leverage to address it. Below, you'll find a powerful process that guides entrepreneurs and companies through a framework for how to use leverage.

Before we dive into the different categories of this framework, I want you to think about your goals. I want you to get clear on what you want. Only then can we start this process because without a clear, definitive goal, we can't find or create the right strategies to get you there. You can always go back to Chapter 2 for reference.

*Write down your business goals below.*

_____

_____

_____

_____

_____

*Then, think about what you need to reach those goals. Is it more leads and clients? Lower costs? Better sales process? More exposure? Restructure your offerings? Equipment? Inventory? A specialized manufacturing process? Write down what you need to achieve those goals.*

_____

_____

_____

_____

_____

*Then, write down the problems, obstacles, challenges, etc., that are preventing you from achieving your goals.*

_____

_____

_____

_____

_____

## The Leverage Framework

Below, you'll find a category for each letter in the word "leverage". And for each category, there are different areas to look into so you can address the problems/challenges/goal(s) you just listed.

**Lessons** – Mistakes, Failures, Successes from Your Peers and Competitors

**Expertise** – Knowledge, Skills, Intellectual Property, Data, Content, Education and Training

**Voices** – Endorsements, Testimonials, Sponsorships, Social Proof, Reviews

**Energy** – Time, Efforts, Team, Culture

**Relationships** – Brand, Goodwill, Trust, Fans, Audience, Email List, Followers, Networks, Connections, Reputation

**Assets** – Land, Property, Processes, Finances, Capital, Cash, Equity, Building Space, Products, Inventory, Services

**Growth Strategies** – Sales Processes, Marketing, Advertising, Referral Systems, Client Retention Methods, Value Ladders, Sales Funnels, Websites, Associations, Joint Ventures

**Equipment** – Facilities, Technology, Machinery, Electronics, Supplies, Tools

For every goal and challenge you listed, go through each category and write what or _who_ could help you overcome the obstacle or achieve the results you want. As you go through this framework, you're brainstorming ideas on how to address your challenge/goal(s) from _multiple_ angles. Note that certain categories may not apply so just skip those.

Let's look at a simple example.

**Goal/Objective:** More Leads and Sales (Like Every Other Business)

**What's Needed:** More Traffic to Website

**Challenges and Obstacles:** Low Budget

Now, we'll go through the list of categories to brainstorm ideas on how to achieve our goal given our constraints and challenges.

**Lessons** – Don't advertise in flyers or billboards because peers have wasted lots of money with no return, optimize website for conversions for leads and sales

**Expertise** – Get consulting for how to improve sales process

**Voices** – Get sponsors from local companies and endorsements from well-known figures in our field of expertise

**Energy** – Hire an agency to run a small social media ad campaign

**Relationships** – Co-host shows with people who already have my target audience, have email list owners promote my company for revenue share, write articles for publications that can reach my target market

**Assets** – Not applicable

**Growth Strategies** – Model competitor A's advertising strategy, create a referral system like competitor B, add a higher-priced option to my offerings similar to a peer, get ideas from competitor C's organic content strategy

**Equipment** – Not applicable

That was a very basic walkthrough to give you an idea of how to go through the process. You'll want to go deep and be more specific when you go through this yourself. Brainstorm as many options as you can and filter down the best ones for your needs or goals. Now, it's your turn!

*#1: Write down your goal/problem/challenge that you're looking to address. Then, write what forms of leverage from the list above you can use to achieve or overcome it. Then, write out what you need to do or who you need to contact specifically to access that resource(s).*

_____

_____

_____

_____

_____

*#2: Write down your goal/problem/challenge that you're looking to address. Then, write what forms of leverage from the list above you can use to achieve or overcome it. Then, write out what you need to do or who you need to contact specifically to access that resource(s).*

_____

_____

_____

_____

_____

*#3: Write down your goal/problem/challenge that you're looking to address. Then, write what forms of leverage from the list above you can use to achieve or overcome it. Then, write out what you need to do or who you need to contact specifically to access that resource(s).*

_____

_____

_____

_____

_____

*#4: Write down your goal/problem/challenge that you're looking to address. Then, write what forms of leverage from the list above you can use to achieve or overcome it. Then, write out what you need to do or who you need to contact specifically to access that resource(s).*

_____

_____

_____

_____

_____

*#5: Write down your goal/problem/challenge that you're looking to address. Then, write what forms of leverage from the list above you can use to achieve or overcome it. Then, write out what you need to do or who you need to contact specifically to access that resource(s).*

_____

_____

_____

_____

_____

This simple but powerful process will make a dramatic impact for your company. Once you approach everything in your business with leverage in mind, you'll be more productive, get better results, and open doors for new possibilities in your business you may never have thought of before.

Remember, we're looking to utilize *other* people or businesses' resources in a way that's beneficial for *all* parties involved. They might have knowledge or expertise you want and you might have something they want.

You don't want to reinvent anything, start from scratch, or have to learn/do something from the ground up if you don't absolutely have to. We also want to get maximum results for minimal input. Like the adage goes, it's about working smarter and not harder, and *leverage* is the key strategy for doing that.

## The 5 Levels of Who

Now let's dive into one of the most important topics of any business—your WHOs. This framework was inspired by the book, "Who Not How" by Dan Sullivan and it builds upon the concept of leverage.

When talking about who, we're talking about people inside and outside of your company. People that make up all aspects of your business. Because ultimately, *people* drive your companies' results—not products or services.

In this section, we'll discuss the 5 categories of WHO to focus on as you grow your company. Here's a graphic to show the different levels.

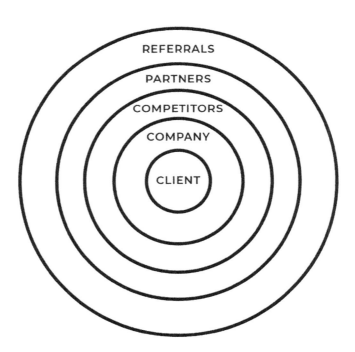

Figure 4.1: The 5 core WHOs to consider in your business

We'll start at the core and then work our way through each level. In later chapters, we'll dive deeper into most of these categories.

## Level #1: Your Clients

The first and most important level of WHO are your clients. They are the people you're trying to reach. They are the ones pulling out their credit cards or transacting business with you. Without clients, there is no business.

One of the biggest pitfalls of most companies' marketing and something I'll help you avoid is not understanding their clients. To optimize your business, you need to know who they are, what they want, and what they don't want. You need to know what their problems and challenges are. You need to know their goals, aspirations, and motivations.

And you need to care *deeply* about them as we talked about with the strategy of preeminence. It's about knowing them better than they know themselves. Many business owners —and even well-established companies—make the mistake of not doing thorough research on their clients.

However, your clients are the *foundation* of all of your marketing and a vital part of your overall business strategy. With most marketing, businesses talk about themselves and how amazing their products/services are. And while that works to an extent, it's *not* the most effective way.

We're all *selfish* beings. We're constantly looking for ways to improve *our* lives. We're looking to survive, thrive, and avoid pain. Recall WIIFM (What's In It For Me) from Chapter 1?

If you can talk to your potential clients and the benefits they seek, you'll perk their eyes and ears and get their attention (remember, AIDA). You'll gain their interest and you'll start the conversation about what you offer.

If you can explain what a client is experiencing better than they can themselves, that'll automatically put you in a better position to connect with them and to offer your products/services. We'll dive more into your clients later in this book because again, it's such an important part of your marketing and business strategy.

## Level #2: Your Business

The next category of WHO is the people that are part of your company. It's all the people that make up your operations, which include your marketing team, your salespeople, administrative personnel, advisors, fulfillment staff, client support, and so on.

This is important because to have the business you want, you need to have the right people doing the *right* things. Hire the wrong people and it can have a major *negative* impact on your operations and your ability to produce the desired results for your company.

When you, as the business owner, hire the right people, it makes your life *easier*. You want to hire people driven and motivated in *their* particular area of genius or talent. They'll be able to use their skills and knowledge to help the company grow with *little* guidance from you.

This also means hiring the right help occasionally, like a business coach to make shifts when needed. Perhaps it's hiring a team to create advertising campaigns to kickstart or propel your company. Maybe it's bringing in a manufacturing or technology consulting company to improve your processes.

This level of WHO is all about the people internally needed to operate and grow your business. But because this book isn't about operations or management, I won't go too deep into it. However, it's an important part of growing any company.

## Level #3: Your Competitors

Moving on, we now have to look at your competition. "Why would we need to look at my competitors?" you might ask. It's because you don't want to operate in a *bubble* (which many businesses do).

You need to know what's going on around you. You need to be aware of what is working for others and also what's *not* working.

If you're in a highly competitive industry, you need to be on the lookout for breakthroughs and threats from others so you're not blindsided or surprised by anything they're doing. That means something that could harm your company or, even worse, put you out of business.

When looking at those around you, you need to be aware of how you can *leverage* what others are doing (in an ethical way). It's also a good way to get an idea of what improvements to make, what potential pitfalls to avoid, and what can give you an advantage over others.

I dive deeper into all the areas you'd want to look into during your competitor research in a later chapter.

## Level #4: Strategic Partners

After looking into your competitors, it's now time to focus on your *non-*competitors. You want to look into people, businesses, or companies that offer *complementary* products/services to your target market.

This is why it's so important to know your ideal client *first* and why they are the first level of WHO.

Because when you do, you'll not only know what motivates them to buy, but you'll also know what *else* they buy and therefore, you can identify WHO they buy it from.

This means you can come up with a list of potential strategic partners to work with to access those ideal clients and potentially build additional revenue sources for your business.

Strategic partnering as a strategy by itself could be a massive source of growth for your company if you did nothing else we talk about in this book. When you partner, you're *leveraging* other companies' products/services, knowledge, client base, expertise, marketing, etc., to expand your own revenue and/or improve your business. Therefore, it's one of the *highest* forms of leverage you can implement into your overall strategy.

One partner could be the difference in earning tens of thousands, hundreds of thousands, or *millions* of dollars in revenue. There's an entire chapter later on that is dedicated to this one strategy with an exercise for finding strategic partners for your company.

## Level #5: Referrals (Your Clients' Network)

The final level of WHOs are the people that your *clients* know. That means tapping into *their* network for more clients and more business.

Referrals may seem like an obvious way of growing revenue for some, but for many, this powerful strategy gets lost in the noise of other client acquisition tactics being promoted out there.

However, referrals have something that other strategies do not and that is the power of *word-of-mouth*—the best form of marketing and advertising there is. And that'll *always* be the case.

Referral marketing doesn't rely on outside platforms which are constantly changing. And there's nothing like an endorsement from a past client to someone they already know sharing *your* products/services. There's already a level of know, like, and trust (KLT) which is beneficial for you!

This shortens the sales cycle and you immediately have some credibility with prospects, which is one of the most difficult things to establish with people who have never heard of you before. Like the previous levels of WHO, we'll dive more into this topic in a later chapter.

## Chapter Takeaways

- Leverage is key to effective growth and business improvement
- The Leverage Framework stands for:
  o Lessons
  o Expertise
  o Voices
  o Energy
  o Relationships

- o Assets
- o Growth Strategies
- o Equipment
- The WHOs that make up your company is extremely important and there are 5 levels to consider:
  - o Clients
  - o Company
  - o Competitors
  - o Strategic Partners
  - o Referrals

# CHAPTER 5

# KNOW YOUR CLIENTS

Much of your marketing efforts and success comes from knowing your ideal market/client. Having a great product or service is important, but it's only *part* of the equation.

If you can't effectively reach and connect with your target audience, they won't ever experience what your products/services can do for them. A common marketing mistake many businesses make is not truly knowing who they serve and therefore, they can't communicate with them as well as they could.

And knowing your clients isn't just about knowing their age, race, income range, or where they live. There's a lot more to it. You need to understand them on a *deeper* level. You must know what drives them, what challenges they face, what pains they have, and what will ultimately connect them to your product/service beyond just the surface-level benefits.

In this chapter, you'll find questions to learn about the people you or your company serves. This is the *foundation* for the rest of your marketing efforts—your website, marketing/sales funnels, emails, advertising campaigns, strategic partnerships, etc.

We'll dive into the who, what, when, where, why, and how so we better understand the people you want as clients. This will make your marketing and messaging extremely effective.

If you can, try and use actual data to answer the questions. If you don't have the data, then you can make educated guesses about your ideal client. This will be better than marketing to no one specifically.

But if you don't have the right information to connect with your clients, then you'll undoubtedly do what most businesses do, which is talk about *themselves*. While this works to a degree, it's *not* the optimal strategy for your marketing and growing your business.

Depending on your company, some questions may not apply, so just skip over them and answer the relevant ones. Ready? Let's get started!

*How old is your ideal client? Give an approximate range.*

_____

*What is their ethnicity?*

_____

*Are they male or female?*

_____

*Are they single, married, divorced?*

_____

*Do they have children? If so, about how many?*

_____

*What is their education level?*

_____

*Who/what influences their buying and/or decision-making? A spouse, their kids, a religion, an organization, etc.?*

_____

*Whose products/services are they using similar to yours?*

_____

*Who do they follow on social media?*

_____

_____

_____

*Who do they turn to for answers to their questions (family, friends, colleagues, partners, etc.)?*

_____

_____

_____

*Who (if anyone) is standing in the way of them buying your product/service?*

_____

_____

_____

*Who is the "villain" in your client's life creating or contributing to the problem they're looking to address? This so-called villain doesn't necessarily have to be someone who has ill-intent and is purposefully trying to harm your clients. It can be a person, a company, an organization, a group, an event, a cultural trend, etc.*

_____

_____

_____

*What do they do in their careers/business?*

_____

_____

_____

*What are their goals, dreams, desires related to what you offer?*

_____

_____

_____

*What is the real result they're seeking related to the product/service(s) you provide? Think deep at an emotional level and what drives their actions and buying decisions.*

_____

_____

_____

*What are the obstacles/challenges they face?*

_____

_____

_____

*What are their biggest pain points? What keeps them up at night?*

_____

_____

_____

*What do they not like about their situation?*

_____

_____

_____

*What is the biggest objection they have to buying your product/service?*

_____

_____

_____

*What is holding them back from getting to the next level (mindset, resources, knowledge, etc.)?*

_____

_____

_____

*What do they enjoy doing for fun or in their leisure time?*

_____

_____

_____

*What groups/associations are they in?*

_____

_____

_____

*What sort of books do they read (personal development, fiction, drama, action, romantic, comics, science fiction, thriller, mystery, travel)?*

_____

_____

_____

*What types of events do they go to (seminars, conferences, networking, art festivals, concerts, social, meetings, etc.)?*

_____

_____

_____

*What do they buy regularly that is related to what you offer?*

_____

_____

_____

*What types of apps are they using the most (games, social networking, productivity, self-help, podcasts, Audible, travel, transportation, shopping, education, sports, music, etc.)?*

_____

_____

_____

*What blogs do they read?*

_____

_____

_____

*What are emotional reasons someone would buy your product/service?*

_____

_____

_____

*What are logical reasons someone would buy your product/service?*

_____

_____

_____

*What are statistical reasons or data can you use to help make a point of why your product/service is necessary in your ideal client's life? For example, if you're selling financial services, you could talk about how X percentage of people don't have enough money for retirement or the average person can only survive on Y years when they retire. This helps paint a picture of a customer's future without your product/service. It doesn't have to be a negative outlook; it can be a positive one. Remember, people primarily do things to move away from pain and towards pleasure.*

_____

_____

_____

*When do they work in their careers or business?*

_____

_____

_____

*When are they most likely to buy your product or service? Is there a specific time of the day, month, or year? Perhaps it's after a major life event like a wedding or graduation, after starting a business, etc.*

_____

_____

_____

*When are they typically using your products/services? Specific time of day, week, month, year, etc.*

_____

_____

_____

*When can they expect to see results from using your product/service?*

_____

_____

_____

*Where do they live? What city, state, or region?*

_____

_____

_____

*Where do they work? Where's their business, office, or company located?*

_____

_____

_____

*Where do they spend their free time?*

_____

_____

_____

*Where do they like to travel to?*

_____

_____

_____

*Where do they spend their time online (Facebook groups, Instagram, LinkedIn, YouTube, forums, etc.)?*

_____

_____

_____

*Where do they get their products/services related to yours?*

_____

_____

_____

*Where do they get their information related to your product/service or industry? Blogs, TV, social media, print ads, magazines, etc.*

_____

_____

_____

*Why do they do what they do? What drives them (money, prestige, legacy, impact, family, community, etc.)?*

_____

_____

_____

*Why would they be seeking your product/service? Are they planning ahead or solving an immediate issue?*

_____

_____

_____

*Why do people buy your products and services? Ask your customers what made them buy from you over anyone else.*

_____

_____

_____

*Why don't people buy your products and services? If possible, find out why people don't buy so you know how to address the reasons.*

_____

_____

_____

*Why aren't they familiar with your product/service? Lack of education, access, etc.?*

_____

_____

_____

*How much income does this person generate monthly or annually?*

_____

_____

_____

*How often does someone use your product or service?*

_____

_____

_____

If there's any other information you think is important to know about your client that may have been missed here, write it down. We'll be using some of this information in other parts of the book.

_____

_____

_____

## Your Client Transformation Journey

No matter what you're selling, your potential client is looking for a result. It's not necessarily the product/service(s) you offer but what it *does* for them.

One of the biggest keys to successful marketing is knowing your client on a *deep* level. And part of that is understanding why they would even consider buying what you offer in the first place.

Why would they go searching for your products/services? What will ultimately make them buy once they've discovered your business?

And often, it's a reason that goes beyond the surface level—it's rooted deep into their core and their being. More than likely, it's motivated by their values and/or their emotions.

Remember this: People don't buy products or services—they buy what it does for them and how it will make them feel. This section will help you determine what your clients are *really* buying. Once you know that, you can then "talk" to those reasons in various places.

In the world of marketing, products/services are often categorized into three *main* areas of life: health, wealth, and relationships. Most of what we do and what we buy is motivated by some factor in at least one of those three areas.

We also make decisions that move us *away* from an undesirable state and/or *towards* a desirable state. These states can also be described as before-and-after or pain-to-pleasure.

Below are several factors/reasons/motivations/desires of what people may be moving away from or towards in those three main life categories. I've also included additional ones based on our most powerful emotions.

Here are the steps...

1. Review the words on the lists and circle/highlight the ones relevant to your specific business/products/services (use your own words if not listed)
2. For your top 10 words, explain how your product/service helps them move away from or towards that state. Pick a few from each

state. For example, choose 6 states they're moving away from and 4 states they're most likely moving towards. You can pick more/less, but 10 is a good number to start.

3. Use this information throughout your marketing materials (website, emails, social media, etc.)

## Health

**Moving Away From:** Tiredness/Fatigue, Weakness, Sleepiness, Unfocused, Too thin, Overweight, Poor Endurance, Hunger, Overeating, Sluggishness, Pain, Tightness, Stiffness, Self-Hate

**Moving Towards:** Energized, Stronger, Awake, Alert, Focused, Healthy Weight, Cardio Strength, Muscular, Lean, Self-Love

## Wealth/Money

**Moving Away From:** Broke, Poor Mindset, Debt, No Savings, Not Investing, No Financial IQ, Active Income, No Retirement Plan/Savings, Financial Stress, Survival Mode, Job or Working 9-5

**Moving Towards:** Abundance, Wealthy Mindset, Debt-Free, Cash Surplus/Reserves, Investment Savvy, Passive Income, Confidence in Retirement, Financial Peace of Mind, Financially Thriving, Entrepreneurship, Financial Freedom

## Relationships

**Moving Away From:** Single, Near Divorce, Divorced, Poor Communication, No or Poor Sex Life, Low Confidence, Poor Family Relationship, No Friends, Feeling Unattractive, Loneliness, Abusive Relationship

**Moving Towards:** Loving Partner, Healthy Marriage, New Partner, Open Communication, Amazing Sex Life, High Confidence, Healthy Family Life, Close Group of Friends, Casual Dating, Finding Soul Mate

## Miscellaneous

**Moving Away From:** Fear, Stress, Doubt, Worry, Anxiety, Anger, Loneliness, Victim Mentality, Confusion, Shame, Helplessness, Complexity, Negativity, Chaos, Dissatisfaction, Lack of Control, Limitations, Hunger, Wasting Time, Overwhelm, Mediocrity

**Moving Towards:** Power, Status, Prestige, Fame, Love, Happiness, Peace, Calm, Joy, Comfort, Security, Simplicity, Clarity, Convenience, Beauty, Knowledge/Wisdom, Hero Status, Control, Freedom, Impact, Positivity, Predictability, Satisfaction, Fulfillment, Reliability, Options, Credibility, Stability, Efficiency, Effectiveness, Productivity, Mastery, Success, Compassion, A Mission

*Write any additional words/state(s) that your ideal client is moving away from.*

_____

_____

_____

_____

_____

*Write any additional words/state(s) that your ideal client is moving towards.*

_____

_____

_____

_____

_____

*In the space below, write down your top 10 words/states and explain how your business/product/service helps your ideal customer move away or towards that state.*

*For example, if my word was clarity, then my explanation could be: This book helps businesses move towards clarity by giving them a step-by-step process to optimize their marketing, create more effective messaging, and provide strategies to help achieve their goals.*

_____

_____

_____

_____

_____

_____

_____

_____

_____

_____

_____

_____

_____

_____

_____

_____

_____

_____

## Chapter Takeaways

- Knowing who your clients are is one of the most important things you can do for your marketing strategy and for your business

- It may have seemed like a lot of questions, but the more information you gather upfront, the better and more effective your marketing will be
- Clients are generally moving away from and/or towards a certain state(s)
- It's important to know what these states are so you can address them in your marketing and have your message resonate with target clients
- Now that you better understand your clients, you can go back to Chapter 3 and update your answers for scaling your business with any new ideas or thoughts

# CHAPTER 6

# COMPETITOR RESEARCH

In today's world, there's really no hiding anything, especially with business. In this chapter, we'll dive into ways you can "spy" on your competitors to advance your company.

Before we do that, let's answer the question of whether or not it's *ethical* to do so. The word "spy" has a negative connotation to it, so this strategy can be a bit misleading. What we're trying to do here is *observe* what others are doing and finding ways to improve your business based on that information.

We do NOT want to copy, rip-off, or steal. Let me repeat that because it's so important to emphasize—do NOT copy, rip-off, or steal other people or business's resources, data, intellectual property, etc.

The goal is to *model* what's working, avoid mistakes/pitfalls where possible, and provide the end-client the best value and experience possible.

Now, while we do want to focus on the competitors that are more "successful" than you, we also want to look at those who *aren't* as successful. And why would we want to do that?

It's so you understand what's keeping them from being more successful and learning what *not* to do. Because no matter whom you look at, you can find lessons that will benefit how you think and approach your own business.

*List your top 5 competitors below.*

_____

_____

_____

_____

_____

Now let's dive into different areas of your competition that you can look at...

## Reviews

One of the best approaches to "spying" is to look at the reviews of your competitors. You can uncover a lot and find some valuable information there. Why?

Because it's *direct* feedback from the clients themselves.

Ideally, look at reviews from third-party websites and not reviews on the companies' own websites. What you're looking for is what people like about the product/service(s) and where the drawbacks or issues are.

If you consistently read that people wish that Product/Service A had a specific feature(s), then it's something to consider for your own products/services. It's also important to look at the positives too—don't just focus on the negatives. That means you want to also look into what clients enjoy or like about your competitors' products/services.

What made them stand out? Why do clients keep buying from them? What are your ideal clients wanting or looking for (i.e., price, value, great client support, speed, durability, etc.)?

By looking into both positive and negative reviews, you're able to understand what's important to your ideal clients so you can improve your own products/services. You can also refine your marketing so it speaks directly to the points that clients actually care about and not just what you *think* they want. This will make your message resonate better and increase your sales conversions.

*List positives you find from reviews that you can incorporate into your business.*

_____

_____

_____

_____

_____

*List negatives you find from reviews that you can avoid, modify, or eliminate from your business.*

_____

_____

_____

_____

_____

## Websites

Next, we can look at your competitors' websites to get an idea of their language, their use of pictures, their content, what they're offering, etc.

If you know these companies are successful, then you want to look into what's helping them and a website may be a big part of their success equation. It's one of the major sources of information for potential clients and it's responsible for much of a business's lead/sales conversions.

As a side note on websites, the *simpler* it is, the better. Many businesses have overly complicated websites that actually *hurt* their business more than help. In a later chapter, we'll walk through a framework so you can build a powerful and effective website.

*List any ideas you believe will benefit your website/marketing strategy.*

_____

_____

_____

_____

_____

## Advertising

If you're spending money on any sort of advertising, then looking at your competitor's ads is a *must*. Especially if you know that it's profitable. One way to know if it's successful is by finding out how long the ad(s) has been running. If it's been running for a while, then it's likely working (unless the company likes throwing money away).

So, what should you look at?

Look into their images, their videos, and their copy. Do they use long or short copy? Do they use bright images? What sort of language do they use? Are their videos value-based or more like commercials? What are they offering in their ads?

Try to understand why it's working well so you can *model* it for your own advertisements. And don't just look at social media—there are so many places businesses can advertise. Look at Google, banner ads, ads in emails, magazine or paper ads, billboards, etc.

Depending on what industry you're in, that's going to affect where your competitors are advertising. And just because we're learning what's working, it doesn't mean you have to do what they're doing to be successful.

You can find ways to *differentiate* but knowing what your competitors are doing can help shortcut your advertising process and improve your results dramatically.

*List any notes about ads that have caught your attention. What was the image, headline, copy, offer, etc., that made it stand out to you?*

---
---
---
---
---

## Sales/Marketing Funnels

So once people see your competitors' ads, where do they go? What process do they take people through to convert them into paying clients?

If possible, can you go through the process yourself to understand what they're doing and why?

Again, we want to *model* the successful, so if a company has spent time and money to test different ways of doing things to find the optimal strategy, you want to leverage that instead of spending the time and/or money yourself.

*List ideas of other sales/marketing funnels or strategies you can incorporate into your own funnels. Look at their headlines, layout, copy, etc.*

---
---
---
---
---

## Offers

Next, look into what other businesses are offering to their clients. Do they offer anything special as an introductory offer or have any unique incentives that help attract more people to them? Do they package their products/services in a way that's more appealing to the client?

When you make offers, the goal is *not* to be a commodity where your products/services are easily comparable to anyone else's. Because if that's the case, there's always someone that can go lower on price and undercut you. And that's not a game any business wants to or should play.

There are ways to avoid that such as building a brand, better positioning, providing more value, and creating client loyalty. You want to differentiate yourself wherever you can and creating more value with your offers is a great way to do that.

*List ideas of how you can improve your offer to match or exceed that of your competitors.*

_____

_____

_____

_____

_____

## Processes

If possible, can you look into another successful business's processes of how they operate so effectively? Do they have specific strategies or methods that allow them to be more efficient, more effective, reduce costs, generate more sales, etc.?

This could be their sales process, their email marketing campaign/style, how they train employees, their content creation process, their client service strategies, etc. There are a lot of areas required to operate a business and a "simple" improvement in each area can have dramatic results on how the business runs.

Although this book isn't about operations or management for scaling a business, it's definitely something to consider as you continue to grow.

*List ideas of where you can or need to improve your processes and what you can learn from others to help you.*

_____

_____

_____

_____

_____

## Fulfillment and Follow-Up

When fulfilling products/services, do your competitors do anything different that helps them differentiate or improve their business? Do they package products in a certain way? Are they adding in special messages? Do they have special delivery options, etc.?

The business transaction is not over when cash is collected. The client experience *afterward* and how the business leads them to the next step is extremely important. A lot of companies are missing this important part in their process. They just expect that people will buy again or refer others to their business because they had a good experience.

Sure, they may, but it's not likely. They need guidance, so you want to make it easier for them to do business with you again.

*List ideas of how others fulfill their products/services and follow up to improve your own processes.*

_____

_____

_____

_____

_____

## Look Outside of Your Industry

When looking at competitors, it's natural just to think of your own industry because that's where you are. But if you're looking to differentiate, you have to look outside. Keep your eyes and ears open as you go about your day-to-day.

Observe every business you interact with and look into how and why they do certain things. What do they do that makes you feel good about doing business with them? What makes you keep coming back as a repeat client versus going anywhere else?

The biggest breakthroughs may well come from this one strategy alone.

*List ideas from outside of your industry you can use to improve your business.*

_____

_____

_____

_____

_____

## Chapter Takeaways

- Many businesses can find a lot of value exploring and learning about the companies/products/services they're competing against
- When you look at virtually every aspect of another business, you're able to see opportunities for improving your own business you couldn't see otherwise
- If you focus solely on looking at your own company in a vacuum, you'll waste time and maybe even money trying to figure things out, whereas you may find answers much easier when you look outside. Again, it comes back to leverage!

- Look into other companies' websites, sales processes/funnels, offers, advertising, fulfillment and follow-up processes, etc. for ideas on how to improve your business
- Sometimes, being creative and just doing something different is what makes you stand apart, which could take your business to the next level. It's much harder for prospective clients to compare you to everyone else when you're in a league of your own.

# CHAPTER 7

# TESTIMONIALS/SOCIAL PROOF/CASE STUDIES

In the chapter where we talked about the leverage framework, the 'V' stood for the *voice*'s category. That includes reviews, testimonials, sponsorships, endorsements, etc. These will all improve your marketing and *undoubtedly* boost your conversions for new leads and clients.

There really is no better form of advertising than word-of-mouth. That will *always* be the case. People trust other people's opinions, even if it's from a stranger. Therefore, you want to use the voices of others to build up credibility for your business and your brand.

When it comes to types of testimonials, *video* will be the best format. That way, potential clients get to see, hear, and even feel what another person experienced with your products/services. This makes it the most powerful and influential type you can get.

If you can get a video testimonial, you can then pull the audio and/or transcribe it for the written version. However, video is often the most *difficult* form of testimonial you can ask for. People are less willing to share their thoughts in front of a camera and have it posted for others to view.

So audio and written testimonials would be the next best options to share with prospective clients. Written is the most common and is what most businesses typically ask for when requesting feedback. So at the *minimum*, ask clients to share their thoughts through writing.

Testimonials can be used in a variety of places and is vital throughout your marketing. They can be placed on landing pages, sales pages, in your email marketing, on your website, throughout your sales funnels, on your marketing flyers, on your social media platforms, and throughout your advertising campaigns.

You really can't have too many testimonials, so the more you can get, the better. It doesn't mean you have to use them all, but it's important to collect testimonials as part of your overall client process.

Again, videos are the best, but written ones work well too. And if you can use a name and even a picture of the person, it'll be much more effective than an anonymous review. For gathering powerful testimonials, here are five questions you can ask your clients:

1. What was the problem/issue/challenge you were having *before* you discovered our product/service?
2. What did the frustration feel like as you tried to solve your problem?
3. What was different about our product/service compared to others you may have tried?
4. How is your life/career/business/relationship/etc. better now that your problem/challenge has been solved or is being solved?
5. Are there quantifiable numbers you can share that tell us how we've helped you? For example, saved a certain amount of money, earned a certain amount of money, lost a specific number of pounds in a specific time frame, etc.

These are just some *starter* questions so you have a foundation of what to ask when contacting clients for testimonials. You can modify them how you see fit. You don't have to use all of them but the purpose is to *guide* clients to give you effective testimonials.

You don't want to leave it open-ended and just ask what they thought or how their experience was. That's too vague and a client likely won't address the right points that will make your testimonials effective for prospective clients. Remember, to get better answers and results, we have to ask better questions. *In the space below, write down your strategy for collecting testimonials from your clients. Will it be asking through email, phone call or message? Will you have a survey or way to collect videos? Brainstorm ideas below.*

_____

_____

_____

*Below, write your testimonials so they're compiled in one area and easy to refer to later on. In the next chapter, I'll share with you exactly where you can use your testimonials throughout your digital marketing assets.*

*Testimonial #1*

_____

_____

_____

*Testimonial #2*

_____

_____

_____

*Testimonial #3*

_____

_____

_____

*Testimonial #4*

_____

_____

_____

*Testimonial #5*

_____

_____

_____

## Other Voices to Leverage

Besides testimonials, other examples of voices include your *peers* who endorse you. That means people in your community or other businesses who will vouch for your company/products/services. It could also be reviews that people left on sites like Google, Facebook, or Yelp. If you have well-known sponsors willing to support your business, that helps build trust and credibility with potential clients too.

Basically, the idea behind using voices is leveraging the experiences or thoughts of anyone that supports your company. Then, using those words throughout your marketing to help people take action. Whether it's to become a lead or make a purchase, the voices of others will have a *huge* impact on people's decision-making process.

Remember the see saw we discussed in the first chapter? Well, it's usually the testimonials, case studies, and stories that past clients or peers share that get people over the edge to make a buying decision. Sure, well-written copy and a great offer help, but it's just part of it.

You need to stack up the reasons someone should make a purchase to outweigh the reasons not to purchase. There are only so many features and benefits you can share. But if prospects can see and hear *multiple* examples or cases of how past clients achieved what they want, then that's ultimately what will get them to act.

## Chapter Takeaways

- Word-of-mouth advertising is one of the most powerful forms of marketing there is
- To improve your marketing and increase your conversions, leverage the voices of past clients, peers, and all the people who support your company and your products/services
- You can use your testimonials in many areas such as your website, landing pages, email campaigns, sales pages, social media, advertising, etc.

# CHAPTER 8

# BUILDING YOUR DIGITAL MARKETING ASSETS

Now that we solidly understand marketing, a vision for your goals, strategies for improving your business, testimonials and more, it's time to build your *online* marketing assets.

This includes your website, landing page, email campaigns, and a sales page. Basically, it's the *minimum* of what a business would need to have an effective online marketing "ecosystem" to generate leads and conversions today.

I've broken down this framework into a process called The Modular Marketing Method™. This method is simple, clear, and effective. We'll be using a lot of the principles and strategies discussed throughout this book.

The process you're about to go through will help virtually *any* business—small operations to larger companies and in a variety of industries—with their online marketing strategy. It's valuable for solopreneurs, coaches, local businesses, internet entrepreneurs, agencies, consultants, digital-based businesses, and even Fortune 500 companies can find value from this process.

Remember that this process is *not* meant to be an all-in-one solution for your digital marketing plan. It's not about getting traffic or visitors to your business. Instead, it's about turning those visitors into new leads and converting those leads into paying clients.

You'll go through a systematic framework to build or improve your online lead conversion and sales process. Whether you're just starting or have been in business for many years, the goal is to increase your *frontend* conversions, which will have a ripple effect and a major impact on your entire business.

The idea behind this approach is that most people or businesses treat each of their marketing assets separately. So they build their website independent from their landing page, their sales page, and their email campaigns. And this results in wasted time, energy, and maybe even money.

Figure 8.1: Marketing assets are typically created
at different times with different strategies.

However, most don't realize there is a lot of *overlap* for much of the content that goes into each marketing asset. What is said on your website can be used in your emails. What's in your emails can also be used on your sales page. What's on your sales page can also come from your website.

Figure 8.2: Your website, sales page, and email campaigns can share similar messaging and should be based on your client.

Most people need to hear the *same* message repeatedly for it to resonate with them. Therefore, the strategy here is to repeat the messages we want our prospects to understand multiple times in multiple places.

In this chapter, we'll be creating "building blocks" or modules of information which you can use in *various* places throughout your marketing. Thus, saving you from confusion, overwhelm, and wasted time trying to understand what to write and where to write it.

Much of this process emphasizes your marketing messaging and your ability to write copy. The words you use throughout your marketing is important. But don't worry, you'll get guidance on how to structure your words and tips for improving your copywriting skills.

Here's how this method is set up...

First, you'll go through a "data gathering" process. This is *the* most important step because it lays the foundation for the rest of the process, so take your time here and think through your answers. Much of this will be from what we've done throughout this book already.

Once we have all the information, we can then build out your marketing assets like your website, lead funnel, sales page, lead magnet, email campaign, etc.

Each question/answer has a unique TAG that will correspond to a specific location on one or more of your marketing assets.

W – Website

SP — Sales Page

LP — Landing Page

TP — Thank You Page

For example, a question with tag SP3 means this answer will go on your Sales Page in the number 3 spot. W4 means that answer will go on your website in the number 4 spot.

Now, if you're not selling something through a sales page, don't worry. You can just skip that part if it's not applicable to your business. Focus on your website, lead funnel, and emails.

For answering the questions throughout this chapter, you want to answer as if you're talking with your ideal target client. Imagine they're sitting across from you and they're asking *you* the questions. Then, just write what you'd say to them.

This is a great *start* to getting clear answers, but we'll work on adding more to it so we can make your answers (and your marketing) much more effective.

When clarifying your message, you want to avoid any jargon (i.e., special words or phrases that might be used in a particular profession).

Unless you know for sure your target market will understand them, you run the risk of confusing people or making them feel unintelligent because they don't understand the words you're using.

It's best to error on the side of being "simplistic" with your words. You want your message to be as clear and concise as possible.

Here's the overall framework for this method. It shows you the digital assets involved and how prospects should flow through it all. It consists of a website, a lead funnel, a sales page, and email campaigns.

A lead funnel's *sole* purpose is generating leads for your business and having people enter your email follow-up campaign. It's made up of a landing page, a lead magnet, and a thank you page. We'll dive more into each one of these later on.

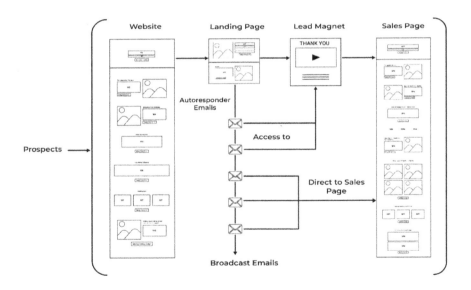

Figure 8.3: How your prospects enter and move through your digital marketing ecosystem.

When writing your answers, just know they don't have to be perfect here. But be detailed and thorough and it will make the rest of the process easier.

## COPYWRITING TIPS

Your ability to create effective marketing is heavily influenced by your ability to write. Don't worry, it's not as hard you think.

Below are tips to improve your copy in a *short* amount of time.

1. **Write as if you're giving advice to a close friend.** That means you might have to be a little stern. Don't be afraid to tell the truth and call the client out at times. You are the advisor and their guide. Sometimes they just need a little push.

2. **Write how you speak.** Sounds basic, but for some reason, when we write, we take on a different voice. Keep it *conversational* and avoid writing like you would for a formal paper.

3. **Don't worry too much about proper grammar.** Focus on the message, the language, and the tone because that's what people will pay attention to.

4. **Have some personality when you write.** Before you start typing, get into an excited state! Excitement will move people to take action.

5. **Use short and punchy sentences.** Don't drag out your points. Like I said before, don't worry about being grammatically correct. You're writing for *conversions*, not for your 7th grade English teacher.

6. **Use emotion-triggering words.** People buy based on emotions and justify with logic. So understand what emotions your target client is after when considering your product/service. Refer to the Client Transformation Journey section.

## BUILDING YOUR WEBSITE

In an earlier chapter, we got a better understanding of your ideal clients. Now that you know exactly *who* you're trying to serve, let's answer questions that will make up the content for your website.

But before we do that, we have to understand a few important things so we can avoid some of the *biggest* mistakes that businesses make. Mistakes, which cost them to miss out on revenue.

Your website is one of your *primary* sources for sharing information with new potential clients. Therefore, you want to make a great impression when they land on your page. You only have a few seconds to capture someone's attention and get them interested in your business. Therefore, you need to be clear and concise about who you help, how you help them, and what you offer.

Most businesses *undervalue* the role of their website within their marketing strategy and its impact on their revenue. Your website is a marketing asset and it should *grow* your business. And that's what we're focused on doing here—turning it into a *sales machine*.

When people come to your website, they generally have a few main questions in mind...

1. What do you do?
2. Can you help me reach my goals/solve my problem/get me results?
3. What should I do next?

So you want to answer those questions concisely without causing any sort of confusion or overwhelm. Make it simple, streamlined, and effective! Here are some of the top website mistakes to avoid:

1. Too many exit points that lead people away from your business
2. Too many options, which causes procrastination
3. Information overload of content that's not beneficial to the potential client
4. Poor layout and design causing poor perception of your business and brand

5. No enticing offer for the visitor to take the next step in your sales process

6. No clear call-to-action(s) guiding people on what to do next

While it may seem counterintuitive, more information isn't necessarily better. Just because you have a lot of valuable content to share, it doesn't mean you should post all of it on your website with *direct* access. Ideally, we want to provide enough information for your visitors to decide if they want to make a purchase and/or become a lead.

Once they become a lead and you've captured their information, then you can *strategically* share your content with them over time. We talked about the importance of the follow-up and the concept of *how* you market matters. So instead of giving people too much information for them to consume on their own where they can get overwhelmed, we want to control how and when they consume it.

That also means instead of putting all of your social media and page links (i.e., about me, contact, etc.) at the top of your website, put them at the *bottom* of the page. Remember, we don't want people to easily leave your website or get distracted from your main objective.

Your website should have multiple buttons so visitors can easily become a lead or client. Again, we're making it obvious and straightforward so people know what to do next. Too many businesses hide their call-to-actions or they have ten buttons leading to ten different places. If you give people too many chances to leave your website, they'll likely take it.

Throughout this process, you'll avoid those revenue-killing mistakes so you can optimize your website and get better results. Now let's start building the foundation and the "modules" of this process! Remember to answer the questions as if you're talking directly to your ideal target client.

# W1

*Create a "One-Liner" or Headline for your business. In a short sentence, summarize what your business does and who it serves. Here's a basic formula:*

*Helping [Target Market] [Result Target Market Desires]*

*This will tell your website visitors exactly what you do in a clear and concise way. Don't try to be too clever or too cute. We also created a one-liner in an earlier chapter so you can refer to that section and then modify based on what you now know about your target client.*

*Examples: Helping Entrepreneurs Scale Their Companies Faster, Easy Marketing for More Profits, Helping Mothers Build a Successful Career at Home, We Help Local Businesses Generate Leads on Autopilot, Helping Doctors Grow Their Practice, We Help Couples Build a Stronger, Loving Relationship*

---

## W2

*Create a Tagline or Sub-headline for your business. You can use a few short sentences or even just one-sentence words to further explain what you do, how you do it, or maybe even some benefits you offer. Try to use 3 phrases or words as there is a rhythm and cadence that makes it effective when reading. Refer to the words you selected in the Client Transformation Journey section.*

### Examples:

*Phrases: Fast Service. Reliable Transportation. Simplify Your Business. Feel More Energy. Quick Results. Trusted for Over a Decade.*

*Words: Bold. Fearless. Empowerment. Strength. Dependability. Clarity. Freedom.*

---------------------------------

---------------------------------

---------------------------------

---------------------------------

# W3

*What is the main problem your business solves? Who do you serve? What are the results they want? Here's where you dive into the main problems or challenges that your target client is facing. You want to amplify the problem and get the person to acknowledge and understand the extent of it as well as the negative impact it has on their life/career/business/relationship/etc.*

*Talk about how "most" of your target market wants to reach this end result, but they're likely struggling because of certain reasons, which you want to explain. TIP: Ask questions that your target client would likely say yes to regarding a result or problem they're likely having.*

**Examples:**

*Do you wish you could [insert a result they want]?*

*Are you tired of [insert a problem they've likely been experiencing]?*

*Struggling with [insert a common challenge they're likely dealing with]?*

*The problem with losing weight in today's world isn't because of X, it's because of Y. Most companies tell you how to do X, but they don't tell you that you also need to do Y if you want to get the results you're after.*

_____

_____

_____

_____

_____

## W4

*Introduce your business here by explaining who you help and how you help them. How do you get your target clients the results they're after? Is it through products, services, consulting, programs, courses, books, etc.?*

*You can also share a bit about why you're helping this group of people (your target client) and why you want them to achieve their goals. This is your origin story, which may help you connect with your target audience.*

### Examples:

*At [insert your company], we offer private coaching programs to mothers over 40 to help them achieve their emotional and health goals. We have strategic frameworks that allow our clients to make breakthroughs in the shortest time.*

*Growing up, we also dealt with extreme mental and emotional health issues. And after dedicating our life to learning and healing ourselves, we made it our mission to help as many women as we can overcome their daily challenges so they can live more free, happier, and healthy lives from hereon.*

_____
_____
_____
_____
_____

## W5

*In this section, dive a bit deeper into what you do for your target audience. Expand on what you mentioned in the previous sections so a visitor knows whether or not you're the business that can solve their problem or address their needs.*

*This is more of an open section for you to talk about what you offer. But don't just talk about what you do. Remember to relate it back to the client's desires, values, and goals so it better resonates with them.*

**Examples:**
*Our unique product/service(s) helps our clients achieve X goal faster so they can save X hours a day and spend that time doing what they love.*

*We're experts in helping clients save money so they can have more funds for vacations/savings/their family.*

*We make your life easier/better by [insert how you do it], so you can enjoy your days more and escape the daily stress and overwhelm.*

_____

_____

_____

_____

_____

## W6

*Explain how your business differs from most others in your industry. What competitive advantage do you offer? Here's where you can use your USP!*

*If you don't believe you have one, then what can you do differently to position yourself away from your peers?*

**Examples:**
*Our unique system does [fill in what it does for the client], which allows them to [insert a benefit they'll experience].*

*Our proprietary method helps our clients [insert the result they want] in less time and with less effort.*

*Unlike most other companies who just do X, we also offer Y and that helps you achieve [insert desired result] faster.*

_____
_____
_____
_____
_____

## W7

*Compile testimonials for your business and/or your products/services. Testimonials help establish trust for your brand/company and they help your target client feel more comfortable knowing that others have had great results from what you offer.*

*Below, compile at least 3 testimonials that will be featured on your website. You can use the ones from a previous chapter.*

*Website Testimonial #1*

_____
_____
_____

*Website Testimonial #2*

_____
_____
_____

*Website Testimonial #3*

_____

_____

_____

## W8

*Make a call-to-action for what you'd like your visitor to do.*

*Hint: It's to go into your lead funnel and get your lead magnet, which we'll talk about later, so we'll come back to this part. Or, it can be to make a purchase if it makes sense for your business.*

*But really quick, your lead magnet is something of value you give away for free in exchange for a visitor's email address/other contact information so you can communicate and market to them after they've left your website.*

### Examples:
*Download Our Free Guide That Will [insert the result/benefit it offers].*

*Get Instant Access to [name of your lead magnet] to [insert desired result].*

*Ready to [insert desired result]? Grab Your Free [name of your lead magnet]*

*If You're Looking to [insert desired result], Then You'll Need the [name of your lead magnet]*

_____

_____

_____

_____

_____

## Your Website Layout

Remember that your website should be simple, clear, and effective. It should also be pleasing to the eye and allow the visitor to easily consume the content on it. Here's a general framework/wireframe that can be used to build your website.

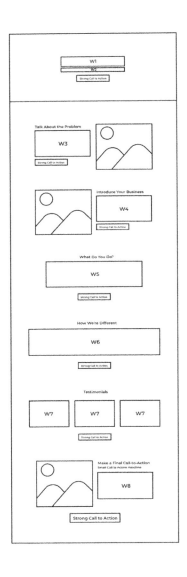

Figure 8.4: A wireframe for the main page of your website.

The information you compiled above can go into its corresponding placeholders in the layout (see the tag above each question). There's a mix of sections for words (which is where your answers will go) and places for images. Your images should be congruent and complementary with the content that it is placed next to or nearby.

Note that this framework is just a *baseline* to start from and is not set in stone. Feel free to get creative and design it to match your needs. But remember, the words on the page are what's most important and having the right information is your priority. This is why the questions you answered above were *strategically* asked—they fit into this marketing "puzzle".

From this layout, you may notice that there isn't an About Me page, a Contact page, or a section to put your social media links. This is contradictory to what many web designers might tell you that you need to have.

Remember that we want a *streamlined* process for converting visitors to *leads* and/or *clients*. Therefore, we want to reduce or eliminate as many distractions as possible so people take the action we want (i.e., become a lead or make a purchase).

You can have your About Me and Contact information on your *main* homepage—no real need to separate them and have visitors do more "work" to get that information. As for a blog, you can provide articles to visitors to share content, educate, and build rapport.

But don't forget our main objective—leads and sales. This is why you want to create your foundation with the framework above—it's already been optimized for your business.

Also, if you've been featured in any media or worked with any major companies that would build credibility and trust with your target market, add those logos near the top of your page under the header. You could also place them in a later section but generally, they're used at the top to establish authority early on with visitors.

## YOUR PRODUCT/SERVICE SALES PAGE

Now that we've compiled the information about your business and clients for your website, we need to compile the content for the product/service that you'd like to promote.

Again, if you're not selling a product or service through a sales page, you can skip this step. However, this section may still help with your marketing message if you're selling through other methods, so at least look through the questions.

For creating a sales page, it's important to have the right content in the right order. There needs to be a flow and a sequence to how information is presented to a prospect.

With a website, it was a little broader in terms of what you do and how you help clients. It was also information that was more so about your business/company in general. Here, we want to get into specifics and really explain why someone should invest in a specific product/service.

Whether you're selling coaching, a book, digital products like courses or templates, physical products, other services, etc., having an optimized sales page that summarizes the problem you're solving, educates the prospect on potential benefits, clearly explains what your offer and value proposition is, and has proof of past results is crucial in converting your leads into buyers.

Just like you did in the previous section, you want to continue the conversation with your target client. But instead of talking about your business like on your website, we're talking more about how your product/service will help clients achieve their end goal or objective.

## SP1

*Like you did for your business/website, write down a One-Liner or Headline for your product/service. Create a simple phrase that explains what your product/service does for your target client. What result will they experience?*

*This will go in the header section of your sales page and is one of the first things someone will see/read, so you want it to stand out and be clear.*

**Examples:**

*The Only Course You Need to Be a Digital Marketing Expert*

*This Book Will Help You Become a Best-Selling Author in Less Than 6 Months*

*The Fitness Program Designed to Get Male Entrepreneurs Over 50 In the Best Shape of Their Life*

---

---

---

## SP2

*Like you did for your business/website once again, create additional tag lines, slogans, or sub-headlines. Use a short sentence or a few words to quickly summarize the benefits of what your product/service offers.*

*This will go in the header of your sales page under your One-Liner/Headline.*

**Examples:**

*Made Just For [insert target client].*

*Lightning Speed Results.*

*Better Sleep. Less Stress.*

*More Sales. More Freedom.*

*Helping You Do What You Love Most.*

*Become the Leader in Your Industry.*

*Passion. Purpose. Profit.*

*Undeniable Results.*

*Hit Your Weight Loss Goals in Record Time.*

_____

_____

_____

## SP3 (Reference for E3)

*Explain and amplify the problem(s) that your product/service addresses. Use questions to get people to identify themselves as the right client for what you offer.*

*Your questions should highlight the obstacles or challenges that your target client has been struggling with for some time.*

*Identifying problems gets people to understand the widespread issues they cause in their life and makes them more open to a solution (i.e., your product/service).*

### Examples:

*Do you ever feel like losing weight is overly complicated? Do you wish you can just get a customized plan that tells you exactly what to do so you don't have to guess and waste time trying all these different things?"*

*Are you tired of buying course after course only to learn a small piece of the puzzle and feel forced to spend even more money? You've been misled to believe that you need to only learn how to do X, but there's more to it.*

*The healthcare industry forces people to pay absurd amounts of money for things they don't need and overpay for what they do need. You could be saving that money for other things like your family, your hobbies, or vacations.*

_____

_____

_____

_____

_____

## SP4

*After you clearly explain the problem that the target client is likely facing, you then introduce your product/service as the solution.*

*What is it and how does it work? Who is this product/service designed for?*

*Share some features of your product/service, such as the number of modules/ lessons, length, what type of content you offer, what's included, etc.*

### Examples:

*This is a 250+ Page Book Filled with The Best Strength Gaining Exercises*

*The [insert name] Course is a 20+ Video Program with PDFs and Assignments to Ensure You Get [insert desired result]*

*The #1 Product for Helping You Build a Doghouse in One Hour Without Any Skills or Tools Needed*

*Introducing Our Interactive Software That Allows You to Cut Your Calorie Tracking Time in Half and Keeps You on Track 24/7*

---

---

---

---

## SP5

*Share the benefits of your products/services. What is the result they want? What does your product/service do to help them achieve what they want?*

*Features are great, but BENEFITS are what sell. And when you're thinking of benefits, you want to go deep and talk about how their overall life and emotional well-being will be improved.*

*Less headache, less worry, less fear, less stress, more happiness, more energy, more fulfillment, more passion, more freedom, more time, etc.*

*Here's a simple formula to help brainstorm...*

*Our product/service has [insert benefit] so you can [how it'll better their lives]*

**Examples:**
*Our product is completely online, so you can save money and time from traveling away from your family/business.*

*This 8-week program will allow you to enjoy less studying and more time with your family and friends.*

*After reading this book, you'll find passion and fulfillment in both your life and career, so you wake up energized each day, loving every moment.*

---

---

_____

_____

_____

## SP6 (Reference for E4)

*Why did you create this product/service? Share a story that a visitor can identify or connect with. Did you have a problem they are now facing?*

*This is similar to the Origin Story of how/why your company was started, but here, it's more direct to the product/service you're selling. Here, you can dive deeper into the beginnings or creation of your product/service.*

### Examples:

*After years of struggling with [insert common challenge], I created [insert product] to help as many single mothers as I could to find their strength.*

*I spent thousands of hours studying and obsessing on how to solve [insert problem] for [insert target market] so they can [insert benefit]. After finding the best research and data, I developed [insert product/service].*

*My brother has been battling [insert challenge] his entire life. I couldn't stand watching him suffer any more, so I created [insert product/service]. Then I realized how many people were in the same situation he was, so I made it my mission to help as many people as possible rid their lives of [insert challenge].*

_____

_____

_____

_____

_____

## SP7 (Reference for E7, E13, E16)

*Like you did for your website, compile testimonials for your products/services.*

*Again, testimonials help establish trust and they have a huge impact on helping your clients move towards a buying decision. You want to include several testimonials in your marketing.*

*Below, compile at least 3 testimonials that will be featured on your sales page.*

*Testimonial #1*

_____

_____

_____

*Testimonial #2*

_____

_____

_____

*Testimonial #3*

_____

_____

_____

## SP8 (Reference for E7, E13, E16)

*If your product/service has case studies, share the results of past clients and how they went from Point A (where your client is now) to Point B (where they want to go, which your product/service will help them get to).*

*Talk about past client's challenges/problems and then how your product/service overcame them to get your client their desired goal.*

*If you can use exact figures or data, this will help (i.e., increased revenue by X%, lost X pounds in Y weeks, got X dates in just one month, etc.)*

*Case Study #1*

_____

_____

_____

_____

_____

*Case Study #2*

_____

_____

_____

_____

_____

*Case Study #3*

_____

_____

_____

_____

_____

## SP9 (Reference for E8)

*What makes your product/service different or better than what's in the market? Is it valuable, better in some way, simpler, etc.?*

*Talk about what others are doing to give a point of reference and then what you do differently that makes your product/service unique and ideally, more effective in getting them their desired results.*

### Examples:

*[Insert product/service] has a special material that keeps your body warmer, so you don't have to wear more layers that restrict your climbing ability.*

*Most medicine promise results in 100 days. Our patented system uses a [insert feature] that allows you to reduce your healing time to just 44 days.*

*Other courses focus only on part of the marketing equation. This course teaches you everything you need to know from A-Z for half the cost.*

*Popular brands commonly use this cheap material that breaks easily and forces you to replace the product in 2 months. However, we use a specially designed fabric that is twice as strong but allows you to use it for up to 6 months.*

_____

_____

_____

_____

_____

## SP10

*So you've explained your product/service, the benefits, why you're better than your competitors. Now, what is your offer?*

*Explain what someone is getting when they purchase today. Share any bonuses or additional value-add items to sweeten the deal.*

**Examples:**

*Today, you'll get access to 6 modules with 30+hours of content, 6 PDF worksheets, and 40+ hours of audio.*

*In this kit, you get Product A that comes with Product B and Product C. As a Bonus for buying today, you'll also get access to a limited collection of interviews from the top pediatricians discussing children's health.*

*Besides Product/Service A, you'll also get Bonus B, Bonus C, and Bonus D to make sure you reach your goals faster.*

_____

_____

_____

_____

_____

## SP11

*Think about objections people would have to buying your product or service. It could be related to price, duration, time to get results, time needed to invest, how would the client know if it'll work for them, etc.*

*Address these common objections to reduce the number of reasons people will "create" in their minds for not buying your product/service.*

**Examples:**

*You may think that 8 weeks is long for a program, but it goes by quickly and it's to virtually guarantee you get the results you're looking for.*

*Some people believe that a thicker cloth means that it's stronger, but it's actually the weaving pattern and the fibers that matters more. We use a thin cloth with a tighter pattern as well as the strongest fibers in the market.*

*$497 might sound like a lot of money, but it's an investment and the low cost of getting a proven system that will help you avoid losing more than that price in the future because of the mistakes you'll likely make trying to go at it alone.*

_____

_____

_____

_____

_____

## SP12 (Reference for E5)

*Compile a set of at least 3 frequently asked questions (FAQs) and answers about your product/service. These can help address objections, but again, the goal is to reduce all of the reasons people would have for not buying your product/service.*

*Preemptively giving them the answers to what they want to know also reduces the friction to buying and lessens the time it takes for them to make their buying decision.*

*Below, write out the FAQ and the Answer in the same box.*

*FAQ/Answer #1*

_____

_____

_____

*FAQ/Answer #2*

_____
_____
_____

*FAQ/Answer #3*

_____
_____
_____

## SP13

*If you have any guarantees you offer for your product/service, write it below. What do you offer to reverse what a potential client would consider a "risk"?*

*Although not necessary, this will help people be more comfortable making the purchase if they feel like there's "no risk" in it for them.*

### Examples:

*If you're not happy with [insert product/service], just send us an email within 30 days of purchase and we'll happily refund you in full. No questions asked.*

*You can test drive the program and if it's not for you, just let us know within 14 days and we'll give you a full refund. And you'll get to keep the PDFs.*

_____
_____
_____
_____
_____

## SP14

*So after a client has learned about your benefits, seen your offer, and you've addressed their questions and objections, it's now time to summarize what you're offering here and make a final call-to-action to purchase.*

### Examples:

*So when you purchase today, you're getting Product A, and bonuses of Product B and Product C. If you're ready to stop struggling with [insert their goal], then act and invest in your future.*

_____

_____

_____

_____

_____

### NOTE:

This is the last question in the "required" list of questions for this section. Remember this is just a baseline and you can use any parts of this framework that you'd like.

These following questions aren't absolutely necessary for use on your sales page, but many questions/answers will be used in your email autoresponder campaign, so you'll need to answer them anyway.

It's up to you whether you want to include the remaining questions/answers on your sales page or not.

## SP15 (Reference for E9)

*Who is the "villain" that is causing your client to experience the problem you're solving for them? This need not be an actual person, company or real entity. It could be a mindset, common behavior, or thought pattern that limits people and keeps them from reaching success. Talk about how this "villain" is holding them back and making your client's life worse.*

*Then, share how your product/service is the "hero" and saves people like your target client. What does your product fight against? What does it fight for?*

**Examples:**
*This book provides people like you with empowerment and the feeling of self-worth while destroying limiting beliefs that hold people from their potential.*

*This program teaches you how to become masters of money and your finances, so you don't fall victim to the "money system" that keeps most people struggling financially their whole lives.*

---
---
---

## SP16

*What is happening in your industry that causes people NOT to get the results they want?*

*Is there a common message or something being taught by your peers/competitors that could actually hurt people or that's preventing them from reaching their goals? Or at least slowing down the process?*

*If so, you want to call them out (not directly) and share how/why this common misbelief actually hurts more than helps. This is a way to position yourself as someone who is honest and wants to "save" your target client from the wrongs of your industry.*

*Examples:*

*You may have been led to believe that you need to limit your caloric intake to X calories. But that's not true. Inside the [insert product/service], you'll learn how you can still eat X calories and lose weight.*

*Most dating coaches will teach you that you just need be confident to be attractive to others. But confidence actually comes second to this one important trait, which we'll dive deep into in Module 3 of the program.*

_____

_____

_____

## SP17 (Reference for E6)

*What's the biggest mistake people commonly make when trying to fix the problem or achieve the result associated with your product/service?*

*Share what the mistake(s) is and how they hurt people's results. Then explain how your product/service helps them avoid the mistake(s) and why it's beneficial for them to do so.*

*Examples:*

*Most people have way too many components to their skin care routine. However, we help you achieve clear skin with just 2 steps, which means less time to implement and less harsh chemicals that other brands use.*

*Most beginners will try to piece parts of the puzzle together, which costs more time, more money, and even more frustration. We give you the entire process in a simple system, so everything is congruent and works together perfectly.*

_____

_____

_____

## SP18

*Why do most people fail in getting the results they want and how does your product/service help them avoid that? Limiting mindset? Lack of belief in themselves? Not finishing the program?*

*Share what prevents most people from getting the results they want and what your product/service does to increase the chances of success of the results they want.*

### Examples:

*Most people fail with other products because they aren't given the right mindset to start with, so they were doomed from the start. That's why we have an entire module dedicated to rewiring your brain for success.*

*The majority of people who buy programs like this fail because they quit too soon. However, we've built out a whole 12-month calendar to generate ideas and stay on track for the long term.*

_____

_____

_____

## SP19 (Reference for E12)

*How will the client's life be better after experiencing your products/services (think health, wealth, relationships)? We talked before about sharing the true benefits of your product/service.*

*Here, we want to paint the picture of how life will be better long into the future. We want to share how other parts of their life will be better as a byproduct because your product/service helped them in a different part of life. So think about the ripple and residual effects of what your product/service can do for your clients.*

*Examples:*

*When your business becomes successful, you'll feel more empowered and confident. You'll be willing to try new things, explore new places, meet new people. Perhaps make new friends, find the true love of your life, and finally achieve the level of happiness you've been searching for.*

*When you restore your body to full health, you'll feel strong and grounded. You'll have more energy to put into your career/business, your hobbies, and into your loved ones to strengthen your relationships.*

_____

_____

_____

_____

_____

## SP20 (Reference for E11)

*How will the client's life be the same or worse if they do NOT purchase your product/service (again, think health, wealth, relationships)?*

*Previously, we talked about the benefits of buying your product/service. Now, you want to explain the consequences of NOT taking action and being stuck in their situation for longer.*

*How is that going to ripple through the rest of their lives and for years to come? Again, you have to think deep on an emotional level and explain how not taking action in one area of life will negatively affect other areas too.*

*Examples:*

*If you keep doing what you're doing, you'll never be able to achieve the fitness and energy level you desire. As your kids grow, it'll become more challenging to keep up with them and enjoy the great moments you'll share.*

*How long are you willing to allow your business to suffer? How long are you going to let your marketing prevent you from more revenue? More income for you and your family?*

*I know change is hard. You might fear investing. But wouldn't it be worse if you kept doing what you're doing and you're exactly in the same poor financial situation 5 years from now?*

_____

_____

_____

_____

_____

## SP21 (Reference for E14)

*What's a negative action that people often associate with the product/service you're offering in terms of what they think they'll have to do.*

*For example, something they believe they absolutely must do but don't want to in order to get the desired result but your product/service can help them get that result WITHOUT having to do that thing.*

*Examples:*

*You may think that to be a great marketer, you have to lie or use shady tactics. But in this program, I'll show you how to effectively market WITHOUT having to sell your soul.*

*Many people believe that to lose weight fast, they need to cut their calories in half and exercise five times per week. With my diet plan, I show you how you can eat healthy portions WITHOUT giving up your favorite foods and snacks. And I'll show you how to create a fitness program WITHOUT needing to go to the gym more than two times per week.*

*Popular opinion is that to attract your soulmate, you need to build this fake confidence. I'll show you how to grab the attention of the person you desire WITHOUT having to "fake it till you make it" or feel like you're being disingenuous.*

---
---
---
---
---

## SP22

*What should the client STOP doing that isn't working to get the result they want? These are things they may have been led to believe is the "right way" to do things but is more likely hurting than helping them.*

*Then explain the problem that what they're doing is likely causing. You may have to be stern here and call people out. List 3+ things they need to stop immediately if they want to get the results they're after. Then we'll position your product/service as the solution.*

### Examples:
*Losing Weight: Stop counting every calorie because you'll go insane. Stop holding yourself back from the foods you love, you deserve to enjoy yourself. Stop with the crazy restrictive diets, you can eat more and still lose weight.*

*Finance: Stop pinching pennies cause that's not how to generate wealth. Stop sacrificing on what you want today so you can save up for the next 50 years. Stop listening to gurus who tell you debt is bad cause it's not if understand leverage, which we'll teach you.*

*Relationships: Stop pretending like it's okay to be alone forever. Stop lying to yourself and telling yourself you're not good enough cause you are. Stop sitting around and waiting for love to fall into your lap.*

_____

_____

_____

_____

_____

## Your Sales Page Layout

Here's a general framework for your sales page. Like your website, your sales page should be simple, clear, and effective. The answers you created above can go in its corresponding placeholders in the layout (see the tags above each question).

Note that this is just a foundation to *start* with—just like your website. Get creative and design your sales page for your needs. Again, the words on the sales page are what's most important and having the right information is your priority. But design, images, and layout do matter as well!

Figure 8.5: A wireframe of your sales page.

If you're creating a sales page to market a product/service, think about creating a sales funnel with upsells and downsells that come after the initial purchase. What can you offer within that *same* transaction to increase your average order value? Refer to Chapter 3.

## CREATING AND OFFERING YOUR LEAD MAGNET

To generate leads, you need to give something of value away for free for someone to exchange their email address or additional contact information like a phone number.

Do *not* offer a newsletter and expect to get great conversions. People don't want more emails in their inbox, so you do *not* want to use a generic newsletter to persuade people to get on your email list.

That doesn't mean you can't send out a newsletter. But it shouldn't be the incentive for getting people to exchange their contact information.

The main goal of a lead magnet (also known as a lead generator) is to get people onto your email/phone list so you can extend the conversation, provide *value*, build a relationship, and market your products/services.

Below, think about what you'd like to offer to people for *free* in exchange for their emails.

Here are tips for creating a great lead magnet:

- It should be easy and fairly quick to consume
- It should *help* your target client move closer towards their desired results(s) or goal
- It can be a video, series of videos, PDFs, templates, blueprints, guides, quiz/survey results, checklist, calendars, etc.
- It should not take *any* time for you to provide after you've created it *one* time. Meaning you shouldn't have to manually give access when someone subscribes to your list. Access to it should be completely automated, which will save you time and energy.

*Write down what your lead magnet is. It doesn't have to be overly complicated or complex, but it should be something desirable to your ideal client. It can be a video, series of videos, a simple PDF, a guide, a blueprint, templates, audio, etc.*

_____

_____

_____

_____

_____

*What result is your lead magnet going to produce for your target client? How are they going to benefit from it? Will they save time, save money, make money, relieve stress, get clarity, etc.?*

_____

_____

_____

Once you know what your lead magnet will be, go back to section W8 to fill out your call-to-action for your website.

Also, let's say you create a valuable PDF as your lead magnet. Put a call-to-action at the *end* of the PDF to tell people what you'd like them to do next. Examples would be to schedule a call, visit a sales page, watch a video, etc.

We want to make it *easy* for people to do business with us. Therefore, adding a clear call-to-action at the end avoids new leads from having to figure out what we want them to do. Same thing if you provide a valuable video. Make sure to let people know what the next step is so there's no guessing.

## CREATING YOUR LANDING PAGE

Your landing page (also known as a squeeze page) is a simple webpage designed solely to collect emails by promoting your lead magnet. Your landing page should make your lead magnet *desirable* for the target client.

Someone who comes to a landing page has only 2 options...

1. Submit their information
2. Leave the page

Therefore, you want to emphasize the importance and the *value* of what your lead magnet is offering. Otherwise, they won't be persuaded enough to provide their contact information in exchange for it. Your landing page should be simple, easy on the eyes, and clear about what you're offering.

It should *not* have your social media handles or any links that would direct people away from your page. The visitor's options are to either submit their contact information or leave the page. Give people too many options and they likely won't do what you want them to do (in our case, submit their contact information).

Ideally, you want to collect a name and an email address. That way, your emails can be more personalized. Some companies will just ask for an email and others may ask for name, email, and phone number.

Just know that the more information you ask from a visitor, the more friction there is for them and the *less* likely they'll opt in for your lead magnet. This could hurt your conversions so you have to consider what you're doing with that information and if you really need to collect it.

## LP1

*After creating your lead magnet, you need to create a strong headline to promote what you're offering.*

*The main goal here is to build desire and curiosity to make people willing to exchange their email addresses. You have to build up the reason(s) for people to take action so think about what's in it for them. A simple formula to follow is...*

### BENEFIT + CURIOSITY

**Examples:**

*FREE Video Shares How to Tell If the Girl You Like Actually Likes You Back and Exactly How to Ask Her Out*

*This Guide Reveals the #1 Mistake Most People Make in Their Diets That Prevent Them from Losing Weight (and Even Makes Them Gain Weight)*

*FREE Report Shares the 5 Secrets of Generating Money Online that the Top Marketers and Entrepreneurs Use and How You Can Double Your Business with It Too*

_____

_____

_____

## LP2

*Create a sub-headline that dives a bit deeper into why someone should submit their email address in exchange for your lead magnet.*

**Examples:**

*Get instant access to the best formulas to grow your business.*

*Get the exact script to make sure she says YES for the first date.*

*Learn exactly how to avoid this diet pitfall so you can lose weight effectively and easily.*

_____
_____
_____

## LP3

*List at least 3 benefits of your lead magnet. How will their life be easier, better, simpler, more clear, more fulfilling, less stressful, less confusion, etc.?*

*You really want to "sell" someone on why they need to get your lead magnet. It could be because it helps them move away from certain pain points or move them towards something pleasurable or the results they desire.*

_____
_____
_____
_____
_____

## Your Landing Page Layout

Your landing page should be clean, simple, and clear about what you're offering in exchange for someone's contact information.

If you can, include pictures of what you're offering to build up the desire for it. Images like a cover of a PDF, a screenshot from a video, etc.

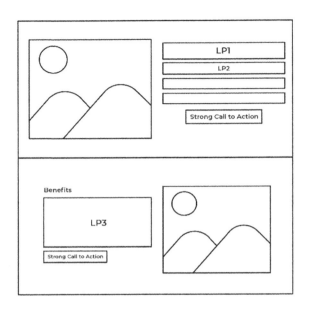

Figure 8.6: A wireframe for your landing page.

NOTE: Your website will be directing people to this landing page through multiple calls to action. Another option is to have a pop-up on your website, so it appears when someone clicks on a call-to-action button to get your lead magnet or they try to exit the page.

On that pop-up window, you can use the same headline, sub-headline, image, and/or benefits that you would on a landing page. That way, they don't have to get redirected to a whole separate page to complete the *same* task of submitting their contact information for access to your lead magnet.

If you have additional pages on your website like a blog, About Me, Contact, etc., promote your lead magnet/landing page link there as well. It shouldn't only be on your homepage.

## Your Thank You Page Layout

The purpose of your Thank You page is to simply thank/congratulate a new lead and instruct them on how to access their lead magnet. You may include any other instructions on this page, such as following you on social media or checking out your products/services.

The reason we didn't want them to do this before was because we didn't want people to easily leave our website without *first* becoming a lead and entering our follow-up sequence.

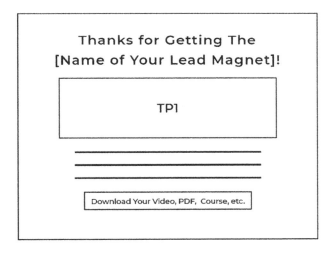

Figure 8.7: A wireframe for your Thank You page.

In the TP1 spot, you can write out what you'd like them to do (i.e., click the button below or check their email). Or you can create a short video to introduce yourself and provide the instruction. This will build a connection with your new leads.

*Write down your call-to-action(s) on your thank you page.*

_____

_____

_____

## EMAIL MARKETING CAMPAIGN FOR LEADS

After someone has submitted their email address for your lead magnet, they'll be getting *strategic*, automated emails that will provide them access to your lead magnet as well as promote your product/service.

This is commonly known as a nurture or an indoctrination sequence because you're teaching and moving a person to change or accept *new* beliefs. That includes beliefs about your company, your product/service(s), and about your lead's situation and what they need to do to improve it.

These emails are sent out *automatically* over a specified schedule. In this section, you will create this set of emails using templates and frameworks to help guide you.

The first couple of emails is mainly to give access to the lead magnet you promised and to share a little about your business/company. The rest of the emails are to *position* your product/service as the vehicle to get them the result(s) they desire and to convert the new lead into a client.

You'll have a variety of frameworks to give ideas of what to write in your emails. Many of these emails are actually based on the answers you created and used for your website and sales page.

The advantage of this modular framework is *leveraging* your content in multiple places to create congruency and consistency in your marketing messaging. The emails will elaborate more on the points you made on your website and sales page(s).

Note that your emails are a *huge* influence in your ability to convert leads into clients. Most sales do *not* come from the initial visit of a website or sales page. Instead, the emails that follow up and share the right messages are what ultimately get people to act.

The emails approach your prospect from *different* angles to help them understand the value of what you offer. Certain emails will resonate better with certain people, so it's important to have a variety to improve your chances of people taking action.

Here are tips for writing your emails...

First, we have to talk about subject lines. You can have the perfect email, but if it doesn't get opened, it doesn't do you any good.

A powerful subject line formula is BENEFIT + CURIOSITY (just like your landing page headline). If you can include a benefit for the reader and throw in some curiosity, that'll increase the chances that a person will click to read.

Here are some subject line formulas you can use to get started...

How to [insert desired goal]

How I [insert desired goal]

How you can [insert desired goal]

The biggest mistake [target client base] makes

Here's a shortcut to [insert desired goal]

The real secret to [insert desired goal]

The fastest way to [insert desired goal]

Another tip is to use *icons* in your subject lines.

If you look at your inbox, which emails stand out to you (if any)? One of the easiest ways to draw eyes to your emails is to use an icon to grab someone's attention. This will help get them to read your headline and then click to open your email. You may not want to do this for every email you send but you should once in a while.

Alright, so people are scanning their inbox and see your catchy subject line and they click the email. Now what do you do?

For writing emails, here are some simple guidelines (many of which come from the copywriting tips mentioned earlier):

- Write as if you're talking to a friend—keep it conversational.
- Don't worry about having perfect grammar. This doesn't mean your emails should be full of typos and errors—keep it clean. But focus on the message, the language, and the tone because that's what people are going to pay attention to.
- Show *empathy* in your messaging. Let your prospects know you understand their pains, frustrations, goals, and desires.
- Be stern with your messaging and do not be too passive. You don't want to "sell from your heels" and you don't want to be timid about it. If you truly believe your product/service can help your prospect, then you have to direct them to take action.
- Make it easy to read (short paragraphs, no run-on sentences, no big blocks of text, don't use a small font size, etc.)
- Study engaging emails you receive in your own inbox and model them

Someone opted into your list. You're the expert/authority/brand. So guide them into taking action. Whether that's watching a video, reading an article/guide, or buying your products/services.

Remember to make it *easy* for the reader to consume the content in your emails. Also, make the call-to-action clear for what you want the reader to do. Don't bury it and make it hard to find.

Once you build out your follow-up email campaign to convert leads to clients, you'll then create an email campaign for those clients to ensure they get access to your product/service and also help them achieve success.

Use your answers from the Sales Page section as the basis for your answers here. It'll save you a ton of time.

*NOTE:*

1.  *Because emails require a lot more writing than other parts of this book, you can either type your emails into a document on your computer or download the supplemental guide at:*

    **thembgplaybook.com**

## Lead Email #1

*Send your lead magnet and briefly introduce yourself/company by talking about who you help and what you do for them.*

## Lead Email #2

*Make sure the new lead gets access to their lead magnet by sending them access to it again.*

*Explain why it's important that they consume it and how it'll help them move closer towards their goals or with their career/business/life/relationship/etc.*

## Lead Email #3 (Reference SP3)

*Dive into the biggest mistake/problem that the product/service you're selling addresses.*

*Explain the problem and how this problem affects different areas of the reader's life. Talk about how it affects their business, their finances, their relationships, etc.*

*Then offer your product/service as the solution to their problem (include a link to your sales page).*

## Lead Email #4 (Reference SP6)

*Share your story about why and/or how you created your product/service. Make sure it's relatable to your target client. Share the problems/frustrations you had and why/how you made a change or a difference. Maybe share how the idea for your product/service was created.*

*Talk about why you help your target audience (i.e., you were once in their position at some point) and explain what your mission or goal is with your product/service and even your overall business.*

## Lead Email #5 (Reference SP12)

*In this email, list out 5+ questions and answers you commonly get about your product/service. If you don't have any, think about questions your target client might have and then provide answers.*

*Or you can work backwards by thinking about the answers you want to give and create questions based on them.*

## Lead Email #6 (Reference SP17)

*In this email, go into the reason(s) why most people don't succeed with other products/services similar to yours.*

*What causes people to fall short of their objectives (ideally, your product/service helps them avoid this reason)?*

*Then, offer your product/service as the solution that helps them get the results WITHOUT the reason most people fail.*

## Lead Email #7 (Reference SP7 & SP8)

*Share a testimonial (or multiple) or a case study about how your product/ service helped a past client. Testimonials have a huge impact on people's buying decision—even if they're from total strangers.*

*We consider other people's opinions more than just relying on the business telling us how great their products/services are. If past clients share their feedback, this will greatly help new potential clients move closer towards buying.*

## Lead Email #8 (Reference SP9)

*Here, you can talk about how other products/services from other companies don't offer something that your product/service does, which helps them achieve their goal faster, more easily, more inexpensively, etc.*

*Basically, you want to position your product/service as superior to others because it offers XYZ features that give your clients certain benefits.*

*Remember to focus on the benefits and NOT the features. For example, don't just say something is lightweight but explain how that helps the client. Like how it reduces physical stress on their back that other products/services typically cause or don't help with.*

## Lead Email #9 (Reference SP15)

*In this email, you can talk about a "villain" that is preventing your target client from the success they want. It doesn't have to be a person or company or some type of real entity.*

*It could be a mindset common with your target market that hinders their success. Then, position your product/service as the "hero" to help them eliminate the villain.*

## Lead Email #10

*In this email, you want to basically run through a checklist to explain who your product/service is perfect for. Your goal is for the person to run down your list and acknowledge to themselves that they meet virtually all the criteria for being a perfect candidate for your product/service.*

*For example, you could say something like…*

*So I just want to make it clear exactly who this [product/service] is for because I don't want you to invest in it if it's truly not for you.*

*But if you're…*

- *Experiencing [insert a pain that your product/service helps solve]*
- *You've been struggling with [insert a challenge]*
- *Constantly feeling [insert some negative emotion]*
- *Tired of being/living [insert something they've been battling for a long time]*
- *Looking for a simple, straightforward way to [insert the promised result]*
- *Someone who wants a step-by-step, proven process*
- *Is an action-taker*
- *A person who wants real change*

*Then, [insert your product/service] is right for you.*

*That's just an example, but hopefully, you can imagine the power of someone reading each line while nodding and saying "Yes, that's me!" to each of your carefully crafted criteria.*

## Lead Email #11 (Reference SP20)

*This email is about painting the picture of what your lead's life will be like if they keep going without investing in your products/services.*

*Go into how their life/career/business/etc., might get worse if they keep doing what they're doing. How will this affect other parts of their life?*

*What pain will they experience because they're choosing not to take action? Then position your product/service as the solution to help them avoid that not-so-pretty future.*

## Lead Email #12 (Reference SP19)

*In the last email, we talked about how life for your lead will be more painful if they don't invest in your product/service. In this email, we're going the opposite way and want to share how life will be better if they do buy your product/service.*

*Again, you want to go into detail here about how other parts of their life will be better off once they achieve the results they're after. Then offer your product/service as the vehicle to help them get to a better life.*

## Lead Email #13 (Reference SP7 & SP8)

*Share another testimonial or case study about how your product/service helped a past client. This is one of the most powerful forms of marketing out there, so use it!*

## Lead Email #14 (Reference SP21)

*This email is about getting the person to realize that they have to stop doing what they think will help them but isn't going to.*

*Maybe it's things others have told them to do, but you disagree and share why it doesn't or will not work. Then talk about what they should be doing to get a specific result and then tie that into your product/service.*

## Lead Email #15

*In this email, you can simply ask if your lead has any questions that you can answer. Whether it's related to the product/service you're promoting or just a general question about your industry.*

*You may not have the right answer, but if you help them find it, that could be enough to get them to invest in your product/service.*

## Lead Email #16 (Reference SP7 &SP8)

*Once again, share a testimonial or a case study (maybe multiple) about how your product/service helped a past client. The more your leads hear about other people's success with your products/services, the more likely they'll consider buying.*

## YOUR EMAIL CAMPAIGN FOR NEW CLIENTS

Awesome, your lead campaign worked and you've got a new client! Congratulations!

Now what? What most businesses do wrong is that once the financial transaction is complete, that's it. They've collected their money and now they're moving on to the next lead to try and convert.

Remember how we talked about preeminence and how we want to be the most *trusted* advisor for your clients? Well, that means we want to continue helping them even *after* money has exchanged hands.

So first, you want to make sure they get access to the product/service. Then, you want to make sure they get off on the right foot towards *success*. Think about what mistakes they can avoid and what will help them achieve their desired result(s). Think about frequently asked questions you can answer *upfront* for your new clients, so they don't have to struggle later.

Remember, I talked about how increasing your clients' success rate plays a role in growing your business in Chapter 3. So it's beneficial to help your clients get the results they're after because it impacts *your* results!

Below, you'll find 6 follow-up email templates to start with but feel free to add more. This is just a foundation to build upon!

NOTE: When someone makes a purchase for your product/service, they should automatically be taken off of your email campaign that is for *leads*. You don't want new clients to continue getting messages telling them to buy if they've already bought. That would overlap with this email campaign which would result in too many emails with conflicting messages. Every Email Service Provider (ESP) should allow you to do this, but how you do it within each software will vary.

## Client Email #1

*Congratulate and thank the client for their purchase. Provide access to their purchase if necessary (i.e., links to PDFs, videos, membership areas, etc.).*

*Reassure them that they made a wise investment by talking about the benefits they will experience after using your product/service.*

## Client Email #2

*Talk about how to get the most out of your products/services for them to succeed.*

*What should they do to ensure they get the results that your product/service promises?*

## Client Email #3

*Talk about common mistakes to avoid so they can once again, improve their chances of success from your product/service. What do clients commonly do after making their purchase that hinders their success or the results they're after?*

*This will help build rapport with your client because it shows you care about them reaching their goals.*

## Client Email #4

*Send a friendly email telling your client that if they need help, they can contact you/your team.*

*This is to help improve their overall client experience and understand that you're there to support their journey and their success.*

## Client Email #5

*Depending on how long it ideally takes for your client to get results with your product/service, you can send out a request for a review/feedback/testimonial. We talked about strategizing ways to get testimonials in a previous chapter and here's an example of where you can do it.*

*This doesn't have to be sent out on the 5th day, so use your best judgement as to when would be the right time to ask for feedback—it'll be specific for your industry. You don't want to ask too soon and you don't want to wait too long where they've forgotten about you.*

## Client Email #6

*Later, you can share more products/services that would be beneficial to your new client. Think about sending them into a new lead funnel with its own lead magnet/email campaign/sales page. Or you can just send them directly to a different sales page.*

*But either way, just keep sending valuable information that would help them!*

## Wrap Up

Congratulations! You've done quite a bit of work throughout this process and you've really set your marketing and business up for success moving forward.

As a business owner or company, you have two options...

You can either learn the skills or you can take what you've created here and find the right people to build out your digital marketing assets (leverage their skills!).

If you hire out the work, you now have a strong foundation of content to provide them. You have virtually all of the right information a web designer, funnel builder, or copywriter, etc., would need to get you the best results possible.

Once you have a solid sales process and your marketing assets such as your website, your sales funnels, and your email campaigns are optimized, then you can focus on directing traffic to your business.

If you create ads, send your traffic to a landing page and base your ad around your lead magnet or a special offer. Don't send traffic to a traditional website where people likely won't take the action you want them to. But if you do, at least you now have a streamlined website from going through this process!

If you start a new business or you're looking to market another product/service, refer to this framework to build your digital marketing assets. It'll save you a ton of time and energy!

Remember, that for marketing, your success will depend on knowing your client. Then it comes down to your messaging to reach, connect with, and getting someone to take action.

Putting the right messages at the right place, at the right time, and in front of the right person will dramatically improve your ability to generate more clients and grow your revenue. And by going through this process, you'll have much clearer and effective messages for your target clients.

And although people aren't reading *all* of your emails, just seeing your name in their inbox is keeping you top of mind. That way, when they're ready to take action, they'll think of you and your company. With emails, sometimes just showing up is what makes the difference between people purchasing from you versus someone else.

## Chapter Takeaways

- The Modular Marketing Method™ is a framework designed to help businesses efficiently create their digital assets that make up their marketing ecosystem
- The information on your website, sales page, and email campaigns overlap, so you can save time and effort by utilizing this framework to create them
- You want your prospects to go into your streamlined system and email follow-up campaign so you can effectively convert prospects into leads and then clients
- Use this method for each new sales page or email campaign that you'd like to create
- Whether you build your marketing ecosystem yourself or hire a company to assist you, this framework will provide the right content to create a powerful "marketing engine" for your business

# CHAPTER 9

# REFERRAL MARKETING

Referral marketing is a *must-have* foundational growth strategy for any business that wants to have *long-term* success.

However, with everything available today for businesses to find new clients, it's gotten lost in the noise of SEO, paid advertising, and all the crazy organic marketing strategies that seem to change every other day.

But word-of-mouth advertising is the most powerful form of marketing there is. When someone sends you a referral, that means they're endorsing you, your company, and your products/services.

That means they *trust* you enough to direct their friends, family, colleagues, peers, etc., to you. And trust is one of the hardest things to build with prospects—especially today.

So what are the benefits of referrals for your business?

- They have a shorter sales cycle because credibility is already established
- They generally ask fewer questions because they're more informed
- They cost less to acquire
- They're more likely to buy

- And they're more likely to send new leads/clients your way because *referrals beget referrals.*

When you have a *strategic* referral generating system(s) in your business, you're building a long-term, profitable strategy for getting new prospects.

However, most businesses overlook or underestimate this powerful strategy and because of that, companies operate well below their potential and they miss out on massive opportunities for growth and scaling.

So what type of referral systems should you have? Well, there are a few ways to go about it. The easiest thing to do is simply *ask* your clients if they know anyone else like themselves that could benefit from your products/services. So just ask. It sounds simple, but most businesses don't do this very basic thing—at least not strategically or consistently.

The big mistake many make is assuming that just because your clients had a great experience with your product/service, that they'll just share it with everyone they know. Like us all, people are distracted more than ever and it's easy for them to get sidetracked or just forget.

Remember how I said that you want to make it *easy* for people to do business with you? Well, you also want to make it easy for them to *share* your business for you. This could be done by asking them verbally in person or over the phone, sending them a message, or emailing them as mentioned in the previous chapter. It's not super difficult, but when asking for referrals is built into your processes, it can have a *massive* impact.

The exact time in terms of days or weeks for when you should ask for referrals will depend on your specific industry/product/service. But generally, you want to ask people when they're starting to see results and are in a state of *excitement.* That's when they're most likely to share your company with their network.

When asking for referrals from clients, you want to describe your *ideal* referral to them. This will generate more *high-quality* prospects. Think about the traits or characteristics your target client has or the circumstances they're in before they would need your products/services.

The more descriptive you are, the more clarity your clients will have so they'll know who would be a great referral.

To take your referral strategy up a notch, you can incentivize referrals through a gift or bonus. Incentives could be a reward—money, a discount on future purchases, points, etc. The industry you're in will determine any rules and regulations you have to be aware of.

While giving rewards for referrals does "cost" you money, you only pay for it *after* a new client has been acquired. So it's no different than spending money on advertising. It's actually *better*. At least here, you only pay when revenue is generated.

The beauty of the referral model is the use of *leverage*, which we've emphasized often throughout this book. For every client you have, they likely know a fairly large network of people similar to them. Meaning they have similar interests, goals, challenges, problems, etc.

So if your business is suited for your client, then there's a high probability they know others that would also be interested in what you offer. One client typically knows *hundreds* of people, so there are at least a handful they can refer to you. However, it does depend on your industry and your products/services.

Let's look at a simple example where each person refers just 2 others. An initial client would refer 2, which would lead to 4, then 8, then 16 and so on.

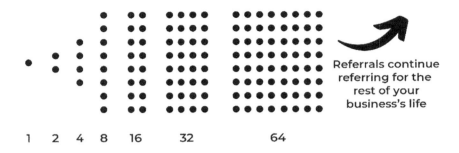

Figure 9.1: Referral marketing can lead to
exponential growth in your business.

Of course, that would be a "perfect world" scenario. Some won't refer any, while others might refer 3, 4, 5 or more!

Now, this is a *long-term* strategy—it's not the latest and greatest marketing hack. Word-of-mouth is and always will be one of the *best* forms of advertising for any business. This is how companies can efficiently grow and not depend on constantly-changing sources of traffic like paid media.

Referrals actually help amplify your paid media results because instead of just getting *direct* revenue from your ads, you'll also get residual and ongoing returns if you have proper referral systems in place.

So if you get 5 new clients from advertising and each of them refers 2 people, you'll have an additional 10 new clients that you wouldn't have acquired if you didn't have a referral system in place. But it wouldn't stop there. Those 10 new clients will likely refer more clients and it keeps going on and on.

This means a better return on ad spend (ROAS) and it's diversifying your lead sources. Paid advertising can help bring in initial clients and revenue in the short-term, but referral marketing will amplify the results over an extended period.

So if your business is operating without at least one referral system, then you should create one *immediately*. Then, think about how you can create another. More referral systems simply mean more opportunities and ways to efficiently grow your business.

If you already have a referral system, ask yourself how you can make it better. How can you make it *easier* for people to send new prospects your way? Remember, this a fundamental strategy that will last the *lifetime* of your business.

Write down at least one referral marketing strategy and how you will incorporate it into your marketing process.

*Referral Marketing Strategy #1*

_____

_____

_____

*Referral Marketing Strategy #2*

_____

_____

_____

*Referral Marketing Strategy #3*

_____

_____

_____

## Chapter Takeaways

- Referral marketing is a foundational, must-have strategy for scaling your business

- Whether you offer professional services or sell physical products online, leveraging the power of word-of-mouth advertising and your clients' networks will make a tremendous impact on your revenue
- Don't expect that your clients will just refer their friends, family, and colleagues even though they had a great experience—make it *easy* for them to share your business for you
- The best time to ask for referrals is during peak excitement when clients are seeing results, so don't want too long after

# CHAPTER 10

# STRATEGIC PARTNERSHIPS

In this chapter, we'll talk about one of the most *powerful* yet underutilized ways to grow your business. It's not creating content, it's not Search Engine Optimization, and it's not running paid advertising.

While those methods are effective in generating new business, they should *not* be the only source for your leads and clients. Here, we're talking about the power of strategic partnerships. This is also referred to as strategic alliances or joint venturing.

As you hopefully know by now, one of my core approaches for growing any business is through *leverage*. That means finding ways to produce a high yield for low input. It also means using other people's assets in a way favorable to *all* parties—not just your own.

We covered The Leverage Framework in an earlier chapter where we looked into various categories of how you can use other people's resources to improve your company. Every business — no matter what you're offering — has a specific ideal client that they're looking to acquire.

As soon you start a company, you're automatically part of a *network* of other companies. And they already market to and service the very same clients you want to attract. Essentially, your client base *overlaps* with their client bases.

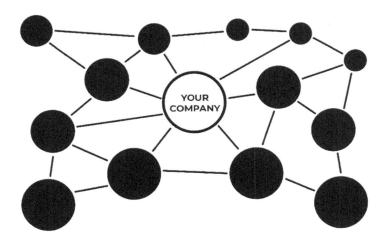

Figure 10.1: Your company is part of a network of other companies who share the same target market.

The key here is to find companies that offer products/services that are *complementary* and non-competing to yours. That means companies that can fill in gaps or fulfill needs where you can't or may not want to.

When looking for a strategic partnership, you want to go into the situation with a win-win-win scenario in mind. Win for you. Win for your partner. And win for the client.

Now, why would you want to work with strategic partners? First, it allows you direct access to your ideal clients with who your partners already have a relationship with. That means you can access many prospects in a *short* amount of time.

Second, it's because prospects directed to your business from partners are like referrals. They come from a *trusted* source, so there's already a level of trust and credibility there. These prospects are more likely to buy than complete strangers. And because they're essentially referrals, they'll likely send more people to your business because again, *referrals beget referrals*.

Here's something *unique* about having strategic partners: As their business grows from all of *their* marketing and strategic efforts, that means more leads and clients they can introduce to your company. And there are similar benefits for them by working with you—it's a two-way street.

When you're partnering, you're *leveraging* another companies' expertise, specialties, resources, personnel, marketing and advertising campaigns, client bases, processes, capital, relationships, etc. You're able to accelerate processes and get results much faster. And it's sustainable if your partners will be in business for a long time.

Now, for creating partnerships, there are several ways you can approach it. You can simply form relationships where you and your partner send referrals to each other. You can offer to pay a commission or referral fee for each client that a strategic partner sends your way. Or you can get creative and generate other types of deals that don't involve money. That could mean exchanging time, services, products, equipment, inventory, etc.

To increase your "market share", which is defined as the percentage of the total sales in an industry that your company or product/service is responsible for, you need to *share the market* with other companies who are complementary and non-competitive.

So how do you find strategic partners?

Here's a simple exercise to brainstorm ideas of who you can partner with for your business. The key is to think about other products/services that your ideal client would buy around the same *time* they'd purchase what you offer.

So, what do people buy *before, during, after, and instead of* your products/services?

Let's look at an example for real estate agents.

**Before:** Wedding Planners, Baby Photographers, Apartment Complexes

**During:** Inspectors, Appraisals, Loan Officers, Painters, Carpet Cleaners, Carpenters

**After:** Furniture Stores, Kitchen/Bathroom Designers and Builders, Interior Decorators, HVAC, Landscapers, Driveway Repair, Pool Services

**Instead of:** Sell by Owner Services, Alternative Real Estate Broker Companies

Now, let's say your company sells health supplements.

**Before:** Exercise Equipment, Gyms, Yoga Products/Studios, Sleep Products, Prescription Medication, Products for Expecting/New Mothers, Acne Products, Counselors/Therapists, Fitness/Wellness Coaches, Doctors

**During:** Gyms, Exercise Equipment

**After:** Gym Equipment, Gym Memberships, Fitness/Wellness Coaches, Dating Coaches

**Instead of:** Medication

Hopefully, those examples helped stir up some ideas for your own business. Below, brainstorm potential partners (industries or professions) similar to the examples above for each of the 4 categories.

*Before*

_____

_____

_____

_____

_____

*During*

_____

_____

_____

_____

_____

*After*

_____

_____

_____

_____

_____

*Instead Of*

_____

_____

_____

_____

_____

For each idea that you came up with, list *specific* companies you want to partner with. Then, you'll want to create some sort of proposition. You need to make sure that it's valuable and beneficial to the business you're looking to work with.

Here are some things to note or ask yourself when brainstorming partner ideas:

- Write the name of Person/Business/Company
- What do they do? What do they offer?
- What's their mission?
- How do their products/services complement mine or how are they related?
- How does my business or my products/services benefit their client base?
- How do I address a need that they can't?
- How can I create a mutually beneficial strategy to market our products/services to each other's client bases?

- Who can I contact to initiate discussions about a partnership?
- What approach will I use to get their attention? Think outside the box or find creative ways of contacting them.

*Strategic Partner #1*

_____

_____

_____

_____

_____

*Strategic Partner #2*

_____

_____

_____

_____

_____

*Strategic Partner #3*

_____

_____

_____

_____

_____

*Strategic Partner #4*

_____

_____

_____

_____
_____

*Strategic Partner #5*

_____
_____
_____
_____
_____

Something to note is that the businesses you're reaching out to should be roughly the same "size" as your business. If you're brand new, it'll be much more difficult (but not impossible) to have a strong value proposition for your prospective partner—especially if they're well established.

Understand that a business may not partner with you unless there's a high potential upside for them. This is not always the case but it's something to consider upfront.

Now, if your business isn't as large as the ones you'd like to partner with, you can find ways to be creative and use *leverage* to make your offer more enticing to your potential partner. Once you have a solid proposition, then contact them!

Will they all reply? Are you going to become partners with them all? Most likely not.

But understand that when you do build these partnerships, your business (and theirs) will ideally reap the benefits for *years* to come. It'll depend on the partnership, but if you and other companies can continue to help each other grow, why would you not keep that relationship going?

And there's really *no limit* to the partners you can work with or have. Unless your revenue is skyrocketing so much you can't keep up with the demand! But that's a good problem to have, right?

Now, this is one of the *biggest* sources (and missed opportunities) of growth for companies trying to scale. And companies with a large client base that are generating millions of dollars in annual revenue are losing out on *millions* year after year because they don't do this one very important business-building strategy (at least not enough).

So if there was just *one* strategy from this book that you take action with and focus on for the rest of your business career that would make the biggest difference, this would be the one!

## Chapter Takeaways

- Strategic partnering is one of the most powerful ways to grow a company
- Partnerships apply the power of leverage through the use of other companies' time, energy, expertise, marketing and advertising strategies, processes, technologies, etc.
- When your partners grow their business through their own efforts, yours grows as a byproduct because expanding their client base means more leads they can direct to your company
- Partnerships can be a simple referral system, a commission or fee-based system, or they can use other forms of incentives or rewards for new client acquisition
- To find partners, think about the 4 main timeframes/categories — before, during, after, and instead of

# CHAPTER 11

# PUBLISHING CONTENT

In today's digital world, publishing content can be a powerful way for attracting attention to your business and generating leads. Depending on the industry and type of business you're in, certain platforms will be better suited than others. We don't want you spending your time on platforms where your ideal clients aren't spending *their* time.

With what you've learned and created throughout this book, you have a great foundation to produce the right marketing messages in your content. But no matter where you're publishing, you ideally want to drive your audience to your conversion-optimized website or directly to your landing page to capture their email address/contact information.

Why? Because you don't own any social media platform and you can lose your account for whatever reason. Therefore, you want to direct people into your ecosystem and your email list, which *you* control. Plus, by capturing emails, you'll be able to send people through your automated follow-up campaigns and generate revenue essentially on *autopilot*.

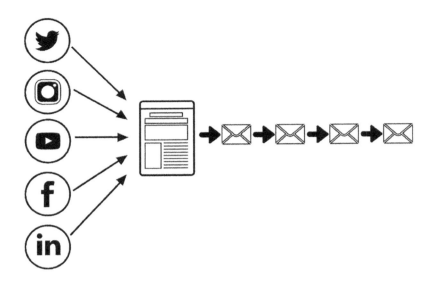

Figure 11.1: Direct people into your marketing
ecosystem which you control.

In The Modular Marketing Method™ section, we built that ecosystem for your business. That means you have a *streamlined* website and landing page focused on directing people into your email campaign, which again, is where the *majority* of sales for businesses happen—it's in the follow-up.

Remember that you can create *multiple* ecosystems for various offers in your company. What you're promoting today might be different than what you're promoting next week. Or you might have multiple offers for different products/services you promote in parallel. Each ecosystem will have its own landing page and email campaign with the main objective of promoting that *single* offer.

## Results-Based Branding

When I say 'branding', I don't mean marketing like big companies where they spend tons of money to "get their name out there." We talked a little bit about branding in the first chapter when we compared it to direct response marketing.

If you're a smaller business, there's a better approach to branding and it's called Results-Based Branding. The foundation of this approach is *education-based* marketing which is providing information about your products/services to help your potential clients make a purchasing decision.

But with Results-Based Branding, we're taking it one step further. Whether you offer a product or service, you're likely helping your clients achieve some sort of *result*. That could be in their life, business, relationships, career, health, etc.

And the best way to show people you can get them results is by actually getting them results! And doing so in *advance*. It's by helping them *before* asking for any money.

It's not enough to just educate people on how your product or service works and why they should just buy it. It's much more powerful and effective if you can actually help people get what they want—or at least part way there.

By doing this, you're demonstrating your value, your expertise, and you're building goodwill and trust, which is a huge factor in people choosing you over the competition.

So when creating marketing content for social media, writing blog articles for your website, or coming up with ad ideas, you want to consider the *result* you truly provide for your target clients. Think about the journey they'd have to go through to get there. And then help them move further along that journey.

We did this in The Modular Marketing Method™ process where we created a valuable lead magnet that was strategically designed to help prospects get results *first*.

Again, you're going to position yourself in a way that is much more effective than just talking about how great your products/services are, which is what many companies do. But that's the *business-centric* model we're trying to move away from.

Here, you're actually demonstrating how your product/service works, why it works, what actions they can take now, and you're building a bond with prospects which will increase your conversions. With your content marketing, make sure your approach is about providing *upfront* value and helping people in advance.

So think about the results you *really* help your target market achieve and the steps they need to get there. Then think about how you can help them go from where they are today to that next milestone. It's the best way for people to know, like, and trust you versus trying to be slick, clever, and/or outrageous with your marketing strategies.

## Messaging Pillars

When creating and publishing content for your business, it may seem pretty daunting and maybe even overwhelming. What are you supposed to talk about? How do you keep coming up with "new" ideas? Well, the truth is (thankfully) that you don't necessarily have to.

You should come up with your *core* messaging pillars. These are the foundational philosophies that represent your business or your company that you can use in your marketing.

When you have your core messaging pillars defined, you can use them on your website, social media platforms, commercials, in your emails, interviews, or for when you're interacting with prospective clients. This will help people know what your business stands for and how it can benefit them.

You want to have a handful of pillars, maybe 3-5. For me, my first pillar is utilizing *leverage* to grow your business. Again, that means other companies' resources such as their time, effort, team, knowledge, processes, skills, capital, systems, audience, etc.

My next pillar is focusing your time on *high-impact activities* you *enjoy* doing and minimizing or eliminating activities you don't enjoy, hate, and aren't the best use of your energy.

And my third pillar is that you need to *care deeply for your clients* and not just see them as a transaction or a dollar amount. That means providing a great product/service to them and looking out for *their* best interests—even if they never do business with you.

If we look at Gary Vaynerchuck as another example, these might be some of his core messaging pillars:

1. You need to hustle and work hard
2. You have to constantly create content
3. And you need to give value to your marketplace before asking for the sale (jab, jab, jab, right hook)

Your messaging pillars are *not* set in stone. They can change and they can evolve over time. But the goal is to find common themes or messages you want to emphasize to your target audience. Then, you can create content with various angles or approaches around those few pillars.

By doing this, you're *consistent* with your messaging and you don't have to come up with completely brand-new ideas for everything you do. Think about your core messaging pillars for your company.

*What are the foundational messages or ideologies that your business has? List them out below.*

_____

_____

_____

_____

_____

_____

_____

_____

_____

*What are the top 2-3 platforms you should focus publishing content on (YouTube, Facebook, Instagram, LinkedIn, Twitter, Pinterest, forums, Quora, etc.)? Think about where your ideal clients are spending their time.*

_____

_____

_____

*What type of content will you post? Use your messaging pillars for inspiration and also use the answers from the Know Your Client section to address people's pain points, challenges, desires, objectives, goals, values, emotions, etc. List your content ideas below.*

_____

_____

_____

_____

_____

_____

_____

_____

_____

_____

## Story Branding

We all love a good story. Especially if it's one we can relate to or one that deeply resonates with us. Building stories into your business and marketing strategy can have a significant impact in your ability to connect to your target market.

Whether it's stories of how your products/services positively affected a client's life or the story of how your business was started, pulling people in through a compelling narrative that your ideal client can relate to is an incredible way to get attention, create interest, and even build desire for what you offer (remember AIDA).

If you want to share the story of your business and its origin or mission, remember to consider the *client* you want to attract and relate the story to their interests, circumstances, or their goals.

As explained in "Building a StoryBrand" by Donald Miller, your company is the guide and your client is the hero. They're on a journey and your role is to help take them through the process one step at a time. Many businesses create stories too focused on themselves. You can do that to an extent but keep your ideal client as the center of the narrative.

This isn't to say you can only create one story. You can (and should) have *multiple* for your business, which you can use in your emails, on your website, or as content on your social media. This gives you a "library" that you can easily pull stories from whenever you're talking to people about your business or your products/services.

When you share stories, it allows prospects to relate or better understand information. As humans, we love when our minds are taken through narratives and if you can craft powerful, relevant stories, you'll gain more attention and get people curious about your company.

Another way to use stories in your marketing is to have different ones for people depending on where they are in their journey. For example, you can have stories for people who aren't yet leads, then stories for people considering their first purchase from your company, and stories for people who want to take the next step on your value ladder.

Remember that when people are checking out your business, they're in "evaluation mode". They're trying to decide whether they should interact and do business with you and they're subconsciously coming up with reasons *not* to (even if they actually want what you offer).

Therefore, your goal is to counteract that natural tendency with reasons they should. And using powerful stories can be the difference maker in moving people to the next step in their journey with your company. Stories can help your prospects relate to past clients, build trust, and take action.

Below, brainstorm or create a story (or multiple) for each section.

*Why was your business started? Here are examples: you had a problem and didn't see a good solution, so you created a product/service, you wanted to improve the way something was being done, you have a mission to help a specific group of people because you were once part of that group (or still am). Remember to relate it to your clients.*

_____

_____

_____

_____

_____

_____

_____

_____

_____

_____

*Share stories of people with great experiences or results from your product/ service. This is more than a just testimonial created by the client themselves. Here, it's more scripted and intentional. You can build a story sharing how a past client went from Point A to Point B, which should be the same journey or similar to the one that your target client will go through. Again, you can create different stories for people at different stages of your sales process to help move them to the next step.*

_____

_____

_____

_____

## Chapter Takeaways

- If you're not creating content for your business in some way, you're likely missing out on revenue and losing to your competitors who are
- Results-Based Branding is about providing value and helping prospects achieve results in *advance* before asking for a sale
- Having a set of core messaging pillars will keep your marketing message congruent and serve as the foundation for your content strategy, so you don't have to come up with "brand new" ideas all of the time
- Stories are a powerful marketing strategy that can help get the attention and interest from your target market
- You can build a library of stories to share on your website, in your emails, on social media, or in conversation when talking with anyone about your business
- You can have stories for prospects or clients who are at different stages in your business that are designed to help them move to the next step in their journey with you

# CHAPTER 12

# SCALE YOUR REVENUE WITH AFFILIATE MARKETING

When growing your business, you need to have the *right* strategies to achieve your goals. And because this book is all about providing ideas for growing your company, I'd be doing you a *disservice* if I didn't share this one particular strategy with you.

Affiliate marketing could potentially be a *lucrative* way for generating more revenue and improving your bottom line. It's also one of the best ways of using *leverage* for scaling a business.

In this chapter, we'll talk about what affiliate marketing is, the benefits of it, and how you can incorporate it into your growth strategy.

Depending on your industry or profession, this chapter may not be applicable. It's geared more towards companies who mainly operate *online* but regardless, the information you'll find here is something to consider. Maybe not now, but perhaps some time in the future.

## What is Affiliate Marketing?

In its simplest form, affiliate marketing is when you earn a commission for referring a sale of a product/service that's created and managed by *another* company. It's a more strategic form of referral marketing, which we talked about previously.

A company that wishes to have their products and services marketed and distributed creates affiliate programs where virtually anyone can join (typically for free) and promote their offers.

However, certain programs do require you to provide information about your company to see if you're the right fit for them. They may look into your social media platforms, your audience, or your business model, to ensure you meet their requirements and that you're a good fit.

Typically, they'll look at candidates with some type of influence, a platform with an audience (i.e., social media, email list), or some vehicle to reach *their* potential clients.

Once you're in the program, the company usually offers training or helpful resources (links, banners, copywriting swipes, email templates, etc.) to make sure you have all the information and tools you need to succeed.

Why? Because your success is also their success!

As an affiliate, you're provided with a special link(s) and/or code unique to you. If someone clicks on one of your links, a cookie is placed on their internet browser. And when someone makes a purchase of a product or signs up for a service (usually within a certain time window), you'll earn a commission for that sale.

Or, if someone is checking out and enters your unique affiliate code, that's also how a company can track who is responsible for that sale(s). Pretty amazing, right?

## Why Do Companies Offer Affiliate Programs?

Well, it's because it's an *efficient* way of marketing their products and services. They're actually using *leverage* by tapping into other people's or businesses' networks to create awareness about their company and to generate sales.

With more traditional means of advertising and marketing (i.e., flyers, branding, paper ads), there are two big *flaws*…

**Flaw #1**: It's difficult to track return on investment

**Flaw #2**: The products/services may not even reach the right audience

A ton of advertising money is essentially *wasted*. When a company uses affiliates, they only pay commissions (i.e., advertising costs) *after* a sale is made. Not before sales like with banners, marketing in magazines, billboards, newspapers, mailers, etc.

Plus, companies get to target people who are more likely to buy their products/services based on the affiliate and their type of audience/client base.

## Benefits of Affiliate Marketing

So, why add affiliate marketing to your business strategy? Here are several reasons and benefits of this model…

- You don't have to create the product/service, which can be time-consuming and require a lot of upfront capital
- You don't have to design a sales page for the product/service
- You don't have to handle the sales process
- You don't have to be the expert; the company will answer questions about the products/services
- You don't have to deliver the products to the end-client
- You don't have to deal with shipping and processing returns
- You don't have to handle client service—the company takes care of that

Those activities are what you *don't* need to do as an affiliate. Many of which are the biggest challenges and bottlenecks in terms of operations and scaling a company.

## What Do You Do as An Affiliate?

Basically, your goal as an affiliate is to send people from your website, social media, email list, etc., to affiliate offers from the parent company. Ideally, the products/services you send your leads or clients to should solve a problem, fulfill a need, or meet a desire. It should also be *related* to what you offer—think *complementary*, non-competitive.

Essentially, you're providing information, giving value, and sharing your affiliate link(s). If someone buys, great. If not, that's okay too. And as an affiliate, it's a super-efficient model and there's virtually no risk (or very little).

It's a win-win-win. Win for the client because they get a product/service that addresses their problem or meets a need. Win for the parent company because they get a new client and only have to pay for advertising *after* they generate sales. And last (but certainly not least), a win for you because you earn a commission/revenue with *minimal* requirement in terms of operations and fulfillment on your end.

You don't have to deal with many of the costly and challenging activities that often come with having your own product or service (as you may already know).

Using affiliate marketing in addition to what you offer can be very *lucrative* and can have a big impact on your growth. If you have your own products or services, promoting affiliate offers can diversify your revenue, so you're not just dependent on *one* stream.

Affiliate products/services could be part of your value ladder. Let's say you offer higher-priced products/services. You may find related, complementary affiliate offers of lower price to introduce to your prospects or vice versa.

So, for those who've come to you but can't afford your prices at that point in time, there's an opportunity for them to still get value and for you to still generate revenue. That way, you're maximizing your ability to produce income no matter what your prospects are in need of or where they are in their journey.

But what you promote does *not* have to be part of a value ladder. It can really be anything that would be *beneficial* to your target clients regardless of its price relative to what you offer as your core products/services.

This model is like a hybrid of strategic partnerships and referral marketing. Although it's not creating a formal partnership, you're still leveraging another company that offers complementary, non-competitive products/services in a mutually beneficial way.

## What Types of Programs Are Available?

More and more companies are offering affiliate programs because of the power in this model for reaching new markets and generating new clients. Most of the major brands and companies you already know and love likely have an affiliate program. One of the biggest (if not *the* biggest) is Amazon.

But there are affiliate programs in virtually every industry — health, fitness, finances, relationships, weight loss, electronics, kitchenware, fashion, and so many more. There are even affiliate programs for software, which is great. Especially ones with *recurring* payments that pay you commissions every single month for making the referral *one* time.

If you go to a search engine like Google and type '[market/niche/specific company] affiliate program' into the search bar, you should be able to find programs that would be relevant and beneficial for your clients. You can also go directly to a company's website, scroll to the bottom, and search for 'Affiliate Program', 'Partner Program', or something similar. They'll usually have a page detailing their affiliate/partner program and offer a way for you to apply.

## Where Can You Use Your Affiliate Links/Codes?

Affiliate links can be used in many different places. From your emails, blog posts, social media, e-books, lead magnets, and even in your product's packaging (more on this later).

If you look at the top earners on YouTube, for example, they typically have affiliate links in the description for the equipment they use to make their videos and the products they're actually reviewing/sharing in the video. Those link clicks and sales really add up!

Plus, they're not even promoting those links aggressively, so it can be a great "passive" strategy for bringing revenue into your business. For blog posts, links can typically be found in review articles or even just throughout the text if any sort of product or service is mentioned.

For example, you'll often find this in food blogs where authors will have links for the ingredients and the equipment they use for their recipes. In general, this is very common in the *retail* space—other popular industries would include fitness and fashion.

## Things to Keep in Mind

Every company has their own requirements and rules with their affiliate program. From the commission percentages, the cookie window, or when and how often they pay out — each program is *unique*.

A pitfall of this model is that if someone clicks on your affiliate link in one browser (let's say Firefox) and a cookie gets placed, but then, they buy using a different browser (let's say Chrome), you likely won't get credit for the sale because the cookie was placed in a *different* browser. And if someone clicks on your link and a cookie gets placed, but then, they click on someone *else's* affiliate link, the other person may get credit for the sale. That's just the way it is.

Also, be sure to follow the terms and guidelines of the affiliate programs you're a part of and promoting. Again, they're all different and you want to make sure you're compliant to remain an affiliate.

## What If You Want to Have Affiliates?

So this entire chapter was about *being* an affiliate where you're promoting *other* companies' products/services. But what if you want to be the parent company and you want to have affiliates marketing *your* products/services?

Well, that's certainly an option! Instead of you leveraging another company and their resources, you're on the "other side of the table" and you're now leveraging the *networks* of other people to market your products/services.

Depending on what business you have, this path may or may not make sense, but it's certainly something to consider. There are always pros and cons to each approach, so it's important to know what your goals are and determine if having affiliates referring you is a strategy you should implement.

*Below, write down and then research 5+ affiliate offers that would be beneficial to your clients and complementary to what you offer. Then write a strategy for how you will offer it (i.e., email, blog posts, YouTube, etc.)*

*Affiliate Offer #1*

_____

_____

_____

*Affiliate Offer #2*

_____

_____

_____

*Affiliate Offer #3*

_____

_____

_____

*Affiliate Offer #4*

_____

_____

_____

*Affiliate Offer #5*

_____

_____

_____


## Chapter Takeaways

- Affiliate marketing is a model where you can earn commissions based on referring sales of products/services for another company
- It has high margins because of its low cost to get started (typically free), no shipping, no purchasing inventory, no fulfillment, no overhead, etc.
- Your primary role as an affiliate is to introduce people to the parent company where they have the systems and processes in place to convert sales, which you'll get credit and the commissions for as the referring affiliate
- There are a variety of ways to promote affiliate offers such as through your website, email marketing, blogs, YouTube, social

media, etc.—just make sure you're in compliance and following the terms of service for each company that you're promoting

- Many of the biggest companies in the world offer affiliate programs, so there's a great chance you can find something that is complementary to your products/services to offer your prospects/clients

- You can also be the parent company where you have affiliates promoting your products/services to their network and marketing your company for you

# CHAPTER 13

# OPTIMIZING BEFORE EXPANDING

Is your business being maximized? Are you getting the most out of what you have? In this chapter, I want to talk about optimization and why it's important to do *before* expansion.

Many businesses focus mainly on more leads, clients, and revenue, but it doesn't mean that what they're currently doing is the best or the most *efficient* way. And if they have a model that seems to be "working", that's all that matters and they push forward trying to scale.

However, when you have a business that isn't operating optimally and you try to grow it, you may be hurting it in a few ways...

- You'll miss out on opportunities for revenue
- You'll *amplify* inefficiencies and problems
- You'll waste money unnecessarily because you'll pay for expenses you shouldn't have to

Let's say you have a car where all of the nuts and bolts were tightened at 75% of what they're supposed to. You're driving along at slow speeds and everything *seems* fine and working as it should. But as you step on the gas and push the car to go faster, the nuts and bolts loosen, components fail, and the wheels come off—literally.

Then, not only is your car likely damaged, but now it'll cost a lot *more* to have the issues fixed that could have been avoided if everything had been checked and done properly to begin with.

With optimization, it's hard to say when things are operating at its peak and when it's a good time to focus on expansion. But most businesses have a certain way of doing things. That's how it's always been done and that's how it will always be.

However, when you take time to optimize, you can find *hidden* areas or opportunities that may allow you to scale revenue much easier and even quicker. Rather than having the mentality of "good enough", we need to shift and ask, "Is this the best way?"

Because optimizing your marketing and your processes with "simple" tweaks could have a *profound* impact on your revenue and your bottom line. And the *sooner* you make optimizing a priority, the better your results will be for years ahead.

A simple rule to consider is the 80/20 rule, which comes from the Pareto Principle. It basically says that 80 percent of the results come from 20 percent of certain actions, causes, or sources. Some may argue that it's more like 90/10 but regardless, there's a smaller percentage of your activities and actions that produce the *majority* of your results.

As your business evolves and you have more "moving parts" or you try different strategies over time, certain things will yield better results than others. So there needs to be this constant, *ongoing* assessment to find out what those high-impact activities are and then put more resources into it. That way, you're getting the most out of every aspect of your business.

You can apply this principle to your advertising, your marketing efforts, your personal time, your employee's efforts, and so on. The idea here is maximizing *everything* you have and constantly fine-tuning, so you're continuously optimizing for the best results.

So where do you even start?

I suggest looking into the beginning of your sales process of when/ how prospects first come in contact with your business. We start here because improvements made early in the sales cycle have a *rippling* effect on the results of every stage thereafter. This could be looking at your social media presence, your website, your advertising, your landing pages. It's addressing your copywriting, your design, your messaging, your offers.

Then, brainstorm ideas of how to make improvements, implement the new or modified strategies for a period of time, review the results, and choose the option that provides the *best* outcome. Then, repeat this process.

After you focus on the beginning part of your sales cycle and optimize it, you can then move on to the next step of your sales process and go through the same methodology. Now, what I just mentioned is focused more on lead generation and marketing.

But other areas that you'd want to optimize include:

- Your sales mechanism (i.e., phone calls, online order pages, etc.)
- Your fulfillment processes for your products/services
- Your packaging if you sell physical products (i.e., can you use less packaging to reduce costs or waste?)
- Your own daily duties and activities as a business owner
- The time to complete all of the major tasks in your business
- Your client service and handling of issues, questions, inquires, etc.
- Your *post*-purchase process for *first-time* buyers to generate more revenue
- Your team members and whether their skills are being optimized

You can even test your pricing and see if lower/higher prices yield better conversions. Higher pricing can actually increase conversion rates so you never really know unless you test it out. How could that be? Well, earlier, I talked about how people associate low prices with poor quality. Conversely, people tend to associate higher prices with higher quality. So if your target market prioritizes higher quality over price, then this could yield better conversions. Again, test it to find out.

There are a lot of ways to improve a business. Therefore, it's important to look at *all* aspects because they all impact each other. Going back to the car metaphor, your business is an *interconnected* assembly of parts. Virtually everything needs to work together efficiently for the whole business to run optimally.

Once you've optimized your business with the assets and personnel you have, then you focus on expansion. But as you're expanding, you're constantly optimizing as you go. Because it's not a one-time or an occasional event—it should be an *ongoing* process that's part of your overall business strategy.

Again, the time, energy, and even money you put into optimizing should generate *more* revenue, make your processes more efficient, and/or reduce wasted resources overall. So it should never be looked at as something *costing* you in any way. It's only costing you if you *don't* do it.

Like using the power of leverage, optimizing means getting the most out of what you have in *all* aspects of your business so you can grow effectively. It's about going beyond mediocre. It's having the "no waste" mindset where everything being done is because it's the *best*—not because it's just how it's been done.

Here's another example: Let's say a sales team handles phone calls and the standard time is 30 minutes. Have you ever tried shortening the call to 25 or 20 minutes without diminishing your conversion rates? If you consistently have shorter calls *without* sacrificing their effectiveness, you can have more calls each day, which leads to more closes and more revenue. Extrapolate those results over time and it makes a tremendous difference.

Or, have you looked at the top salespeople to find what they're doing or saying differently that can be taught to others to improve their results which in turn, improves the results of the whole company? Again, small changes in one area can make a massive impact on the whole system.

Let's say you sell a suite of physical products. Have you looked at your top sellers and your worst sellers to see what to focus more of your efforts on and which ones to reduce or maybe even eliminate? Are their products with extremely low sales taking up warehouse space that your top-selling products could be utilizing?

Again, you want to look at *every* aspect of a business and ask yourself if there's a better way or if things can be done more efficiently and effectively. Because no matter what type of business you operate, there's likely *multiple* areas or ways you can optimize or improve it.

Understand that no two companies are the same. And no frameworks, processes, blueprints, etc. are going to produce the same exact results for every single business that uses it. Therefore, it's important to constantly refine your strategies based on your own company.

*Write down areas that you need to optimize immediately that will make the biggest improvement in the results for your business. What can you test right away that will make an impact on your results (i.e., website, landing page, email campaign, offers, sales funnels, lead magnet, client services, fulfillment strategies, etc.)?*

_____

_____

_____

_____

_____

*Write down other areas of your business you can optimize and continuously improve upon. How often will you refine your strategies to improve your results?*

_____

_____

_____

_____

_____

## Chapter Takeaways

- It's important to optimize your business and strategies *before* expanding because you can amplify issues or problems that may cost you more time, money, and energy later on
- You could also miss out on opportunities for revenue as you scale if you don't have a streamlined website and follow-up campaign, a referral system, or maybe even affiliate marketing as part of your business strategy
- You have to make testing and optimizing part of your business strategy before and as you scale up

# CHAPTER 14

# THE DUAL PARTHENON BUSINESS GROWTH MODEL™

In this chapter, we'll summarize some of the strategies you've learned throughout this book with a concept called The Dual Parthenon Business Growth Model™. It's a concept that virtually *every* business should reference when looking to grow their company. And it's my take on Jay Abraham's Power Parthenon Strategy but with my own personal twist.

Before we dive into the model, let's first recap the 3 ways to grow any business...

1. Increase the number of clients
2. Increase the average cart value or revenue/transaction
3. Increase the frequency of transactions of each client

When you understand those 3 fundamental ways, you can expand your thinking beyond just acquiring more leads and clients. And while having a pipeline full of new leads is a *must* for any business, when you understand other ways of generating revenue, you can make dramatic shifts in your strategy and therefore, your results.

Let's say you had 1,000 clients that purchased a $100 product/service from your business and they did that 2 times over their lifetime. That would be $200,000 in revenue. Now, if you increased each variable by 10%, the total revenue would be $266,200. That's an overall increase of about *33%*.

If you increase each variable by 20%, the total revenue would be $345,600, which is an overall increase of about *73%*. That's the power of *geometric* growth. And while this example is based on *one* product/service and you can make tremendous growth by focusing solely on it, there are other strategies to consider.

Actually, having only one product/service and only one source for new leads puts a business in a very *vulnerable* position—one that you do not want to be in.

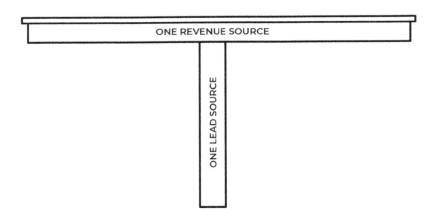

Figure 14.1: A business with one revenue and
lead source is weak and not stable.

Why is this dangerous?

If your revenue is based only on one product/service, this can cause it to fluctuate significantly month-to-month. Something could happen to your lead source and your entire business would be in jeopardy. A competitor could come in with a more desirable product/service and take your clients. Do you see the problem here?

To build a well-rounded and powerfully structured business that produces more *predictable* results and has more growth potential, you want to expand your sources for new leads as well as expand your revenue-generation methods.

Depending on your actual business type and industry, it will be easier for some than others. But the overall concept is *diversification* for leads and revenue. It's important to think *broader* and not be tied to any single source that could easily be affected by things *out* of your control. That means events or conditions that could put your business in danger, or even worse, close your doors.

Below, you'll find The Dual Parthenon Business Growth Model™.

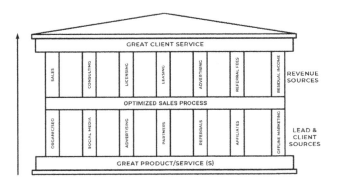

Figure 14.2 The Parthenon represents a strong
structure to model your business strategy after.

We'll start at the bottom and work our way up. As a foundation, you must have a great, valuable product/service. If you don't, then it's the *first* thing that has to be addressed. Because to be in business for the long run and to generate *repeat* business, having an *exceptional* product/service is required.

Next, we have your sources for leads and each pillar represents a source. Here are various ways to generate more clients…

- Advertising
- Direct Mail
- Guest Appearances on Shows, Podcasts
- Keynotes
- Social Media Marketing
- Search Engine Optimization
- Word-of-Mouth
- Referral Marketing
- Strategic Partnerships
- Publications
- Other People's Email Lists
- Live/Virtual Events
- Blogging
- Forums
- Influencer Marketing

Next, we have an *optimized* sales process for converting leads to clients. So, as you're getting leads from various sources, you're able to maximize your ability to convert them. And in The Modular Marketing Method™ section of this book, we went through a whole process for creating a website designed for conversions and building an ecosystem to turn prospects into leads and paying clients.

If you're converting leads to clients at 10% and have a reasonable amount of inbound traffic to your website, imagine if you were converting at 20%. That *doubles* your results if nothing else changes. Now extrapolate that over years and years and the difference in your business is significant. Remember, we covered the importance of optimization *before* expansion.

And imagine if you had a strong *backend* to your business. That's where the power of *geometric* growth can really affect your overall results. This again, is why we spent so much time on your digital marketing assets earlier in the book (website, lead funnel, sales pages, email campaigns). They're such crucial components to your whole marketing and business strategy.

Next, we have your revenue sources. That includes:

- Traditional Product/Service Sales
- Referral Fees
- Commissions
- Consulting Fees
- Speaking Fees
- Advertising for Other Businesses
- Licensing Fees
- Leasing Fees
- Affiliate Marketing Commissions

Your options for revenue will depend on the type of business you have, but these are just some ideas to consider for expanding your company.

To top off this model, have a great *follow-up* process and amazing service to ensure happy, satisfied clients that come back again and again while also *referring* others to your business (through one of the strategies you created in the Referral Marketing chapter).

Most businesses do *not* follow-up enough with their leads let alone their clients. It's usually *one* transaction and then the business is off looking for new prospects. Remember that the third way to grow a business is to increase the *frequency* of transactions for each client. And those additional transactions will happen because of strategic, *continuous* communication with your clients.

Again, the *fortune is in the follow-up*. That means converting new leads into clients and then offering additional products/services on the backend while also providing value at the same time. I see too many businesses *sporadically* following up and when they do, it's just to promote.

So, I may not hear from a company for weeks and suddenly, I get an email asking me to buy something. Often, I don't even remember who that person or company is because it's been so long. I don't know about you, but for me, it's a major *turnoff* and it makes me want to immediately unsubscribe from their mailing list. It's like that friend or relative who calls every few months out of the blue when they want something from you—don't be that person/business.

It's important to deliver value to your clients *regularly* so that when you do make an offer, your clients are more open to it because you've been top-of-mind and you've been helping them in some way—not just reaching out when *you* want something from them.

You've spent a lot of time, energy, and perhaps money to acquire your leads and clients. Therefore, you want to generate the best return on your investment (in an ethical and beneficial way to your clients). So it's important to keep that connection with your clients by serving them while promoting to them.

Now, the goal of this Parthenon model is *not* to build it overnight or create it right from the start of your company. But it's to slowly expand your lead and revenue sources over time. Understand that the more pillars or "moving parts" you add to your business, the more complexity you add as well. It also means there'll likely be *opportunity costs* for investing your resources (time, energy, money) in certain areas over others.

One strategy might sound good in the short run, but it could prevent you from a better strategy (and better results) in the long run. This is something to remember as you expand or pivot and allocate your resources to new strategies in your company.

But if you're looking to scale your revenue and grow your business, this is a model you can refer to for building a more *stable* and consistently growing company. Depending on which sources for leads and clients you choose, know that just *one* of them could lead to a *massive* shift in your business—especially with the right strategic partner. One guest appearance on a show or podcast, one referral system, and/or one joint venture could yield *exponential* growth.

Now imagine if you had multiple lead sources and *each* grew geometrically. What would that do for your company? It'd be pretty astounding.

I hope you can see the power of The Dual Parthenon Business Growth Model™ and why it's so important for virtually *every* business to consider.

Like an actual Parthenon, this is a structure that takes *time* to build. It isn't necessary to use all of these strategies from the start as it can be overwhelming and even lead to growing *too* fast beyond your business's capabilities. But you want to view this structure as a guide to build a solid, stable, and ever-growing company.

*Write down your sources (current and future) for new leads and clients.*

_____

_____

_____

_____

_____

*Write down your various sources for revenue.*

_____

_____

_____

_____

_____

## Chapter Takeaways

- The Dual Parthenon Business Growth Model™ is a model that summarizes how a business should be structured so they're not dependent on a single source of leads or revenue, which makes them vulnerable

- By diversifying, you're able to build a more stable business that can grow faster and more predictably

- A major key to your success is having a *consistent*, strategic follow-up process that focuses on providing value to your clients so you can promote additional products/services over time

# CHAPTER 15

# GENERATE MORE PROFIT FROM PACKAGING

Let's talk about eCommerce and retail goods. This book is about business growth strategies and while it's not focused on a specific industry or type of business, I thought this chapter was necessary because there is so much opportunity being missed for small and large companies.

With physical products, the majority are packaged and shipped to clients with some sort of an external shell such as a cardboard box or a bag. Tens of millions of packages are being processed and delivered every single *day*. That means millions of clients are excited to get their new goods delivered to their door—it might even be the highlight of their day!

The big question, if you sell physical products, is how can you leverage your packaging to grow your company?

Let's say you have an eCommerce business and you only sell your products *online*—you do *not* sell anything in a physical store. Therefore, you wouldn't need to invest heavily into fancy packaging because people are *not* making a buying decision based on it. They're buying through your website or your sales page.

So, you could use your packaging to market the next product or provide instructions on what you'd like people to do after they receive their order. That doesn't mean your entire package should be one big marketing or advertising piece. You can still have your branding on there.

For example, you could use one face of a standard shipping or packaging box and make an offer or tell your new client the next step. That next step could be to re-order, check out other products you offer, claim a bonus, opt into your email or text messaging list if they haven't already, etc.

Here's the thing: You're already creating, labeling, paying for, and shipping these packages/boxes. Why not *leverage* them and turn them into revenue-creating assets? You want to *maximize* that physical "real estate" and use it to grow your business.

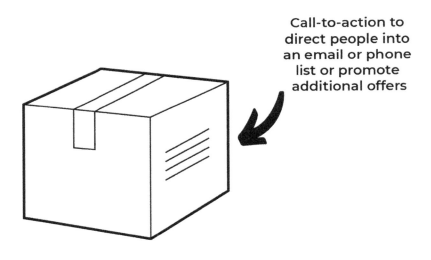

Call-to-action to direct people into an email or phone list or promote additional offers

Figure 15.1: Use one side of your package to instruct people on what you'd like them to do next.

Now let's say that you do sell in physical stores and your packaging *does* have to "sell" your product. Meaning, your packaging needs to catch people's attention and help persuade a potential client to make a purchase. In that case, you'd want to have a flyer/card(s) *inside* of the package that directs the person on what to do next.

Instead of telling people to visit your general website, whether you're selling online or in stores, make some sort of *offer(s)*. Actually, most businesses don't make *any* offers with/inside their packaging. But it's offers that get people to take action.

Instead, most companies just provide a receipt which is very *transactional*. Again, one of the main goals of this book is to be *strategic* with your marketing and business growth approaches. It's also to view your relationship with clients beyond just transactions—it's a *relationship*.

When you send orders to *first-time* buyers, share a special note or a thank you letter that shows your appreciation for their business. Tell them you understand that they have a lot of options and that you're grateful they chose *your* company over all of the others. It helps build a connection with them and makes them feel special—a small gesture like this goes a long way in the eyes and mind of a new client.

So, here are the top 4 things you want the client to do when they receive their order...

1. Buy more of what they bought (if it makes sense)
2. Buy something else you offer (other products in your line-up or value ladder)
3. Buy products that another business offers where you can earn a commission (i.e., affiliate marketing) or you can get paid to advertise on their behalf
4. Refer your product to their network of friends, family, peers, etc., and ask them to share your business for you

Ideally, it's a combination of at least 2 of those strategies—the more, the better.

For example, you could offer a discount on their next purchase or free shipping on another order over a certain dollar amount. You could make an offer for a complementary product you sell. You can have a special referral offer for other people they introduce to your company.

Again, we're trying to make it *easy* for people to take another step in your business. That way, you're not relying solely on them to do what you want them to do—you're being more *proactive* and guiding them, which will greatly improve your business results.

Figure 15.2 Inside of your package, include a flyer/card(s) that instructs the client to take another action in your business (i.e., opt into a list, purchase again, refer others).

If eCommerce stores and retail brands made this shift in their packaging strategy, it would have a *dramatic* effect on their business. And this is even true for larger brands and companies such as Nike, Adidas, Apple, Sony, IKEA, Samsung, etc.

Think about how much packaging they produce and ship to consumers daily. Think about the opportunities there are for other high-quality, *non-competing* companies that would pay them to advertise on or through their packaging to access their client base. This ties in with the concept of strategic partnering.

Here's a great example of how a few companies used this strategy extremely well to better illustrate this whole concept...

I was looking to buy a microphone for my digital camera and was doing normal research like most people do. After comparing several online retailers who had the *same* product at the same price, I made my purchase from Best Buy because they were offering a special promotion to Shutterfly, the company that offers printing services (albums, books, décor, etc.). I've heard of Shutterfly before since they're well-known in their space, but I've never actually purchased anything from them.

So what did I do when I needed a present for an upcoming holiday? I used my special promotion to order that gift and Shutterfly got a new client. Then, when I got my order from Shutterfly, the packaging included a few other items. They had very enticing *introductory* offers for 3 other companies—a popular wine delivery service, a major food delivery service, and another retail business.

For each company, there was a small card with a unique code I could use to get their introductory offer. It was Shutterfly's *affiliate* code. So, if I made a purchase with any of those other companies, Shutterfly would get the credit and the commission/revenue.

Here's something important to note: Even though the affiliate offers didn't appeal to me personally, I immediately thought about *who* I knew that might be interested and I could share these cards with.

And a friend of mine eventually claimed the introductory offer for the wine delivery service. So that company tapped into *my* network even though I'm not their client and they generated more sales!

And remember how we talked in an earlier chapter about why companies can make such appealing, low-priced offers to acquire new clients? It's because they have a strong *backend* and know that the majority of new clients who take the introductory offer will continue to purchase, which increases the lifetime value (LTV) of each client.

Therefore, they can break even or even "lose money" on the frontend because they know their revenue and profits really come from the backend. But because those companies were using affiliate marketing, they didn't have to pay for advertising costs until *after* sales were generated for their company—very efficient and effective.

So I bought *one* item from Best Buy and that led me to Shutterfly, which then led me to 3 other companies. This chain could have continued on if the wine delivery company my friend ordered from did the same thing as Shutterfly did and provided offers to *other* products/services as an affiliate. But they didn't.

So that wine delivery company is not implementing the very strategy they used to access Shutterfly's clients (which led my friend to them) in their own packaging. That means they're missing out on *major* opportunities for growth when you consider how many wine boxes they ship and deliver daily.

Millions and millions of dollars of potential revenue are *lost* each year for so many retail companies because they're not utilizing this *one* strategy in their marketing and packaging.

Best Buy didn't have to ship any additional items but was able to incentivize me to buy through them by giving me a *better offer* than what other retailers could. Shutterfly didn't have to change their packaging, they just had to add in some strategic marketing cards for other companies that had their unique affiliate code—no additional shipping cost for them.

And the other companies that marketed through my Shutterfly package didn't have to pay for any advertising until *after* they acquired a new client (they probably did have to pay to make the cards that went into each package which is minimal).

This example shows the power of strategic partnering as a way to *leverage* other companies' products/services to reach new clients. And it also shows how you can add additional revenue streams by recommending other companies as an *affiliate*. These are ways of adding pillars to each level of your Dual Parthenon Business Growth Model™.

So, I hope this concept and example has sparked some new ideas for how you can better maximize your packaging to generate more revenue. Again, it's about *leveraging* what you already have to get everything you can out of it.

Below, write out ideas for how you can improve your packaging to grow your business. Think about the 4 things you want your client to do and how you can incorporate that strategy.

*How will I get my clients to order more?*

_____

_____

_____

_____

_____

*How will I get more clients to enter my email or phone list?*

_____

_____

_____

_____

_____

*How can I promote other companies through affiliate marketing or advertising?*

_____

_____

_____

_____

_____

*How can I get my clients to share my product/service/company with their network?*

_____

_____

_____

_____

_____

## Chapter Takeaways

- Millions of packages are being sent and delivered to clients every single day
- One of the biggest areas for missed opportunities lies in the packaging for physical goods
- Build a connection with new clients by sending them a special thank you note with their first orders (Note: it doesn't have to just be first-time buyers; this can be done for every time someone receives an order, so they always feel good about their purchase)
- You can scale your business by strategically using your packaging to get clients to order the same or different products you offer, opt into your follow-up system, purchase other companies' products to earn commissions, and/or refer your business

# CHAPTER 16

# QUICK REVENUE PRODUCTION FOR ESTABLISHED BUSINESSES

If you have an established business—perhaps generating 6 to 7-figures in annual revenue—and are looking to generate more cash flow right *now*, here are the top 3 places to start. Note that this is more of a *short-term* strategy and while it'll work again and again, you still want to have a long-term game plan in place.

Here's the list starting with the "easiest"…

## 1. Make Offers to Your Current Client Base

Since these people have already bought from you, this will be the path of *least* resistance because they already know, like, and trust you. And hopefully, they've experienced great value from your products/service(s).

Usually, people stop buying because *you* stop asking. It's not that they don't like what you offer or that they didn't have a great experience. Life happens and they may have just gotten sidetracked or distracted. Maybe they were planning on coming back or buying again but just didn't get around to it.

Sometimes people just need a little reminder that you exist. And when you give it to them, this can produce a surge of new and even *ongoing* revenue once they return to your business. And you could approach this in two ways…

First, you can sell them the *same* thing they already bought. So, if it's something they need again, this will be the simplest thing to offer because they've already experienced it.

You can make an offer for a one-off purchase or maybe even create a discounted bundle offer. This will help your clients save money, generate more upfront revenue for you, and lower your costs to fulfill.

Second, you can offer your clients something *new*. But because it's new, it might be a bit trickier to get them to try it out. So you can offer special perks or bonuses as a reward for being your clients and to incentivize them to purchase. This also allows them to be part of a "special group" who can get first access before the rest of the market.

Something new doesn't mean you have to create it. You can promote offers from other companies through a joint venture or strategic partnership. It could also mean using affiliate marketing to generate commissions. Again, it should be relevant and beneficial to your clients.

If you've run a successful campaign to your client list in the past, try it again! If it's been proven to work, that's where to start—we want simple and effective.

## 2. Get Referrals from Clients

The second strategy to drum up some business quickly is to get referrals from your clients, which we've talked about before. Similar to why people don't buy more from you, the reason companies don't generate enough referrals is that they simply don't ask—at least not enough.

You already have a connection with your clients and if what you provide is valuable, then your clients would be happy to share your business, which can generate more revenue in a *short* time frame.

Usually, it's just a matter of asking and then providing *easy* ways for a client to share your business. Help them understand who your ideal prospect is (who is most likely to buy right now) and then give them directions on the best way to share your business.

Hopefully, you already have strategic referral processes in places, but sometimes, you need to send reminders for the people that have never done it.

## 3. Convert Your Unconverted Leads

The third strategy is to make offers to people who've engaged with you but haven't yet bought. This means they're either on your email/phone list, they're on your ad retargeting list, or you've interacted with them in some way.

They already know you and like you (at least to some degree). You can make them a *special offer* to get them to try your products/service— perhaps a *more* enticing offer than what you made to them originally. That could mean providing a discount or adding additional product/service(s) to sweeten the deal.

Or, you can even offer something else that is complementary. Maybe the timing isn't right for them to buy your product/service but it may be the right time for a product/service from another company that you can share with your leads as a strategic partner or even as an affiliate to earn revenue share or commissions.

## The Fortune is in the Follow-Up (Once Again)

I've said it repeatedly but I can't stress how important it is! If you look at this list, we're essentially going after your hot and warm audiences first—

people who already know your business to some extent. We're starting with the *shortest* sales cycle.

We're *not* trying to get new business from complete strangers—that's the most difficult approach and has the *longest* sales cycle. So it's not about pumping more money into advertising or posting more content. It's not about putting out more offers to a *cold* audience (strangers).

It's about leveraging what you've already built that got your company to where it is today. If you've built your business through advertising, then it's maximizing return on ad spend by increasing your client lifetime value. You've already paid for the leads and clients, so look there *first* before spending more money to acquire new leads and clients.

Most business owners are missing on tons of opportunity because they're so overwhelmed, distracted, or fixated with just getting *new* people to their business. And because of that, they overlook the "low hanging fruit" that lay before them—their client list.

You have to consider the assets you already have first before trying to create new ones. More often than not, business owners are *underutilizing* what they possess and therefore, their companies are performing below their potential. They're constantly looking for the next best thing or the new shiny object when the *best* approach is so close to them they can't even see it.

Now, for creating offers, here are a few tips that may help…

- Create a "special offer" meaning it's not your standard offer
- Provide a reason you're making this offer (i.e., holiday, special event, your birthday, their birthday, liquidating inventory, etc.)
- Add urgency to your offer (i.e., time or quantity limit)

Another strategy to consider is creating a calendar where you make various offers for major events throughout the year. That could include holidays like Valentine's Day, Memorial Day, Labor Day, Thanksgiving, etc. It could also be based on *current* events happening around a specific point in time. There doesn't *have* to be a specific reason but it can help.

Make sure you're *consistently* making offers to your client base *while* continuing to acquire new clients—basically, keep following up! And don't just send emails every few months asking people to buy as mentioned in an earlier chapter. You want to keep in *constant* contact with clients and provide them value at the same time—even if it's just once a week. That way, people are not turned away because each time they get an email from you, it's just a pitch to buy something.

Note that the strategies mentioned here are *generic*. Because there are so many business models out there, I tried to find ways that would apply to virtually *all* companies. But what you can offer and how often depends on your industry and your products/services.

Certain things can be promoted frequently while others cannot. It may be inappropriate or even *offensive* to keep asking people to buy if it doesn't make sense. This is where having a value ladder or affiliate products/services can help—you're not just promoting the same thing over and over.

Again, this is a *short-term* strategy. Make sure you have a long-term game plan for consistently following up with a mix of value and offers for your client base.

*Below, write down ideas for different offers you can make to your client base to generate more revenue right now. Think about all of your own products/ services and affiliate products/services. Think about what you can re-package or bundle to create a "new" offer.*

_____

_____

_____

_____

_____

## Chapter Takeaways

- The 3 quickest ways to generate revenue in your business are to make offers to your clients, get referrals from your clients, make new or different offers to your leads
- The key is having a long-term follow-up strategy that prioritizes your relationship with your clients—don't just send emails every few months when *you* want something from them
- Keep in constant contact with your clients and leads by providing them with valuable content and then make offers between

# CHAPTER 17

# WHAT IS YOUR ACHILLES' HEEL?

When COVID-19 began in early 2020, the world economy was *permanently* affected. No one could have seen it coming. No one could have truly prepared for it. Most industries and businesses were hit hard while a *small* percentage actually benefited from the pandemic.

But that event sparked the idea for this chapter. As mentioned in the introduction, this book isn't about operations, culture, or management—it's about business *growth*. But this is such an important topic I felt like it needed to be included as part of a small business's overall plan.

Referring to a Greek idiom, an Achilles' Heel represents a *weak* spot despite overall strength that could lead to a downfall. No matter what company you operate, small or large, it's crucial to reflect and consistently examine your business and how you're running your operations.

You need to know any flaws or vulnerabilities as soon as possible and create contingency strategies so you can continue to operate smoothly should anything occur. This could be potential flaws or issues in your marketing or advertising strategy, your team, your business model, your products or services, your internal processes, your client service, and so on.

While it's not the most appealing topic, preparing for the *worst* situations — no matter how unlikely — is important whether you're a company with hundreds of employees or a company of less than 10.

What if a key person on your team gets sick? What if they leave? What if *you* get sick? What happens if your ad account gets shut down? What if a certain expense continues to rise and what will it do to your margins and cash flow? Will the company be okay if a specific machine or equipment stops functioning today?

There are so many things that can happen that could put your entire operations at *risk* and it's important to have a game plan ready to execute. As your business grows, the last thing you want is something catastrophic go wrong and then not have a plan ready to address it.

So, I'd like you to think about your business and every major vulnerability or weak spot you have. Think about the worst-case scenarios and work your way through *all* aspects of your business. I know it's not a fun exercise, but if there's anything this pandemic has taught us, it's to prepare for the absolute *worst*.

Many businesses close because they lack cash flow, and they don't have a plan ready to execute when major shifts in the economy or market happen. They don't know how to adapt or pivot because of changing environments or because a new competitor has entered the market and introduced a product/service that is superior to theirs.

Just look at some of the biggest companies you've grown up with and maybe even loved, but they no longer exist today. No one would have *ever* thought they would disappear in their lifetime because they were "too big to fail". But they failed to plan and they failed to pivot.

You have to be proactive and not just reactive. You must look at tough situations and expect that it *can* happen to you. Think more at a macro level and look at the big picture.

What can happen that will put your operations at risk? What can happen that will put your company out of business in the next 6 months or *less*?

It's a scary thought that no one wants to think about and understandably so. But it's *necessary*. Especially as your company grows and your team continues to get bigger, you have more livelihoods to consider.

This is where you need to be *strategic*. This is where you need to be a forward-thinker and look at what's *out* of your control so you can change and manage what's *in* your control.

For every worst-case situation you come up with, you need to have a plan you can quickly deploy. People on your team should also be part of this process. Look to them for where they might see vulnerabilities you can't since you aren't working in those areas day-to-day.

Every person should understand what needs to be done if a certain scenario happened. They also need to know what to do if *you* cannot fulfill your duties as the leader.

It's like buying life insurance. Nobody wants to think about their own demise even though it's inevitable. And if they do pass unexpectedly, the family usually suffers and is financially burdened. It's also why we do fire drills. It's not likely to happen, but it *can*. Therefore, everyone needs to know what to do if it does happen.

Remember, if you fail to plan, you plan to fail.

Now, I'm not saying your business is guaranteed to fail. And hopefully, with the strategies you have in this playbook, you won't. But it's important to think about what could cause it to fail and then plan for it.

I hope this chapter brought to light an *overlooked* but important part of growing a business. It's crucial that you take time to reflect and create contingency plans for the future. And not just planning for more revenue or growing your company but also planning for the potential challenges and vulnerabilities that come with it.

Below, write down the top 3 (or more) weak spots of your business. Where are you vulnerable? What could jeopardize your entire business? Look at your products/services, personnel, pricing structure, sources for revenue, sources for leads and clients, bottlenecks, etc. Then, write a plan for each that would help reduce/avoid the negative impact if those events occurred so your business can continue to operate smoothly.

*Weak Spot/Contingency Plan #1*

_____

_____

_____

_____

_____

*Weak Spot/Contingency Plan #2*

_____

_____

_____

_____

_____

*Weak Spot/Contingency Plan #3*

_____

_____

_____

_____

_____

# CHAPTER 18

# COMPOUNDING CASH FLOW

Hopefully, with the help of this book, your company will thrive and you'll be able to enjoy the journey. Now, what if the revenue and income you generate from your business today could pay you *repeatedly* for the next 10 or 20 years or more?

In this chapter, we're going to briefly dive into a simple yet powerful model to understand the flow of money from and *beyond* your company.

Your business is the foundation and the *catalyst* for your financial future. What many entrepreneurs neglect to think about is the big picture and *residual* effects of their business for their short-term and long-term financial success.

It goes beyond your profits and your income *today*. The goal here is to build an overall strategy that allows you to invest and re-invest your money into *assets* that continue to grow and provide you with cash flow for *life*.

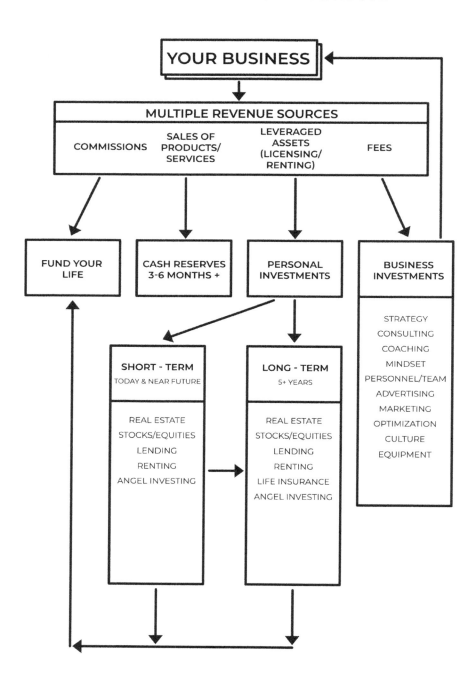

Figure 18.1: The Perpetual Income Growth Model for Entrepreneurs

## Passive Income and Residual Income

Before we dive into this model, let's first understand different types of income that you could earn from your business.

First, we have traditional/active earned income. This is where you're trading your time directly to generate revenue. Wage workers and the majority of employees are paid on an hourly or a salary basis. And while there's nothing inherently wrong with this model for earning a living, it's not ideal as a business owner.

After all, many business owners start their companies to have more control and freedom in their lives. They want more options and the ability to spend time doing what they want when they want. Maybe their entrepreneurial journey is driven by more impact, mission, and purpose. Or perhaps they want to support their favorite charities or organizations.

Regardless of the reason for starting your business, the key to more options and spending time where you want comes down to your ability to use leverage so you're not consistently trading your time for your income.

Passive income is money you or your business earns from little to no effort. To create a passive stream of income, there's usually upfront work you have to do to get it up and running. And you'll likely have to do things here and there to maintain the flow of income but overall, it's very little effort.

If you remove yourself from the daily operations but your company can still run (and even grow) effectively without you, you're earning passive income. You're leveraging systems, processes, and other people's efforts to create revenue for your business. Other examples include collecting income from real estate properties, fees from anything else you rent out, investment returns or dividends from stocks/equities, income from partnerships, or even earning money from a blog.

Residual income is continuing to earn money from a *completed* project or service. It's a form of passive income and it's the most *powerful*. Examples include earning royalties, licensing fees, book sales, and revenue from digital assets (i.e., online courses, templates, blueprints, etc.). Money earned from investment accounts and joint ventures can also be considered residual income.

If you think about musicians and actors, they often earn income for many years (even for the rest of their lives) from the films, movies, and songs they produced *one* time.

While residual income may be passive, passive income isn't always residual. Both types are ideal because you're not actively trading your time for money. And even though passive income is great, residual income is *better*.

And if the amount of passive income you're earning is large enough, you can generate a certain level of financial security in your life. If you couldn't work for an extended period of time for any reason, you can feel safe knowing that your income and cash flow won't stop. This will improve your peace of mind in knowing that your family is taken care of should something happen to you.

Now that we know the different types of income you can earn from your business, let's dive into the perpetual income model.


## Cash Reserves

The first part of the model is your business. It's the engine that feeds the *entire* system. And with it, you want to essentially fund 4 *major* categories.

We'll start with cash reserves since it's the easiest to explain. Every busy should have money set aside that allows them to cover at least 3-6 months of operating expenses with no revenue coming in—the longer, the better.

These reserves could cover overhead costs, unexpected shifts in your business, prepare for a natural disaster, or to withstand an economic downturn which is *inevitable* for any business that operates for many years. It's just part of the overall economic cycle you have to consider and prepare for.

When you have a cushion of cash set aside, you can operate with less stress, you can make better decisions, and you can have more freedom to operate without the crushing fear of running out of money in the near future to fund your business operations.

Now, you don't have to build this reserve all upfront. You can allocate a percentage of revenue to your cash reserves until you hit your goal—perhaps on a weekly, monthly, or quarterly basis.

Again, 3 months at the *minimum*, 6 months is ideal. If you can do 12 months, that's even better. Note that as your business grows, so will your expenses. Therefore, the amount of cash reserves you'll need will also increase so that's something to consider—it's a sliding value.

## Business Investments

These are necessary to help grow or improve your business and include a variety of things such as investing in consulting, coaching, marketing, advertising, updating your infrastructure, investing in your team, or even in assets that produce cash flow for the business such as land, buildings, equipment, etc.

This is important because you'll always want to invest in what will help your business perform better and/or expand, so the other categories below will benefit as well.

Therefore, you don't want to look at these as expenses since the main objective is to give you a return on your investment in some form—even if it's not monetary.

## Fund Your Life

This is the money you need that allows you to live the life you desire for yourself and your family. It means having money for housing, food, vacations, hobbies, transportation, etc.

You want to get clear on how much money you need to make in your business to live the way you want to live. From there, you can work backward and create your business goals and targets (which we did in one of the early chapters)—or at least factor it in.

If you need to make $100,000 each year to fund the life you want, your business strategy will look very different than if your goal is to make $500,000 or $5 million. That's why it's extremely important to know how much it'll take to fund the life you *really* desire.

Now, we don't want the money that funds your life to come from *just* your business. We want them also to come from the next category.

## Personal Investments

Here, we can break this down into 2 sub-categories, which are short-term and long-term.

Short-term investments produce cash flow from now and through the next 5 years and long-term investments produce cash flow beyond the 5-year mark, which could be 10, 20, or 30+ years from now. These numbers are not exact nor are they *the* rule. They are just to differentiate between short and long-term.

The investments you make will depend on your goals, amount of capital, risk tolerance, and so on. Options include investing in real estate, stocks or equities, bonds, lending, life insurance, and even angel investing to name a few.

Now, your short-term investments ideally provide you with income you can use to fund your life *today* and provide a surplus that will allow you to invest in longer-term strategies as well. And that's in *addition* to the income that is being earned directly from your business.

The arrows in the image help you understand the flow of cash through each category.

Now, this book isn't about investing and where you should be putting your income. The goal of this model and chapter is for you to understand the importance of your business in your overall financial picture and strategy.

The better your business operates today and moving forward, the more income you'll have later on because of the *compounding* effects of investing. When you invest, you're using the power *leverage*.

It's what the rich do very well that the middle and lower-class do not. They focus on creating income-producing assets that generate cash flow, which they then put into other assets that do the same. They keep repeating this process and through leverage, they're able to quickly increase and compound their cash flow and their net worth.

So making an additional $10,000 or $100,000 in your business annually can fuel your investments (business and personal) much faster and have a major impact on your financial situation *decades* from now. And that can allow you to work less in your business or give you the option to let go of your business if you choose. That's really dependent on your goals and what you ultimately desire.

If your investments can fund your life and continue to grow over time, then you won't have to work in your business out of necessity. You can work in it because that's what you *want* to do—you have that option.

## Think Like an Investor

A shift you may have to make as an entrepreneur or business owner is to think like an *investor*. I talked about it many times throughout this book, but the key to effective and profitable growth comes from using *leverage*. And that's one thing that smart investors use to consistently produce incredible results and returns on their investments.

When assessing investment opportunities, they look at:

- Potential upside and returns
- Potential downside and risks
- How much capital they need to invest
- The time it would take to produce the returns
- The opportunity costs of each option

They're focused on investments that have a high probability of providing consistent growth and/or high yield opportunities.

Savvy investors are great at finding low-priced or undervalued assets, putting capital (or other resources) into it, and then reaping the rewards after a period of time. They weigh *multiple* investment options to determine which is the best use of their capital and resources.

In business, that translates to finding underutilized, low-cost, or low-input opportunities that produce high yields. The advantage you have in your own business is that you have more *control* of the "engine" that produces the results.

That means you have control over your inputs (i.e., time, money, personnel, etc.) and the mechanism that produces the output (revenue). If you compare this to investing, investors usually can't control the system or vehicle they're putting their funds into. Their results are usually in the hands of someone else or another business.

So, when you're making decisions for growing *your* company, make sure that you're strategically weighing your options and comparing them as if you're an investor. Ask yourself which option is the best use of your time, energy, capital, resources, etc., that have the highest chance of success and that can produce high yield with low risk.

The same is true for your team and personnel. What are they putting their time and energy into and is it the best use for them to get the most optimal results for the overall team? You have to look at each individual in your organization and leverage their strengths and what they enjoy doing.

If you think of your business as a high-performance machine, every person in it is a vital "component" to its ability to operate at its maximum potential. If people aren't being utilized to the best of *their* ability, then it's a waste of their time and their talent.

As your business evolves, your team members will too. They'll learn new skills and take on new roles and responsibilities. So it's important to be aware and make sure they're not outgrowing their role or being underutilized. If so, you have to make adjustments.

This is where you, as a business, have an advantage over an investor. *You* have the control and you can make decisions and take actions that can change your results. Often, an investor can only sit back and *hope* the business or investment they pour their capital into delivers on what they promised.

When you think like an investor, your filters for making decisions improves. You can easily identify what are high-value activities to focus on. For activities that aren't the best use of your time, you can delegate them.

If you do this in your business, you'll consistently make better decisions to fuel your company's growth and performance. Will you always make the right or the best decisions?

No. Just like investors don't get a positive return on every investment or they get less than anticipated, you won't be right 100% of the time. No one is. But also like an investor, one decision could be the "game-changer" that drastically and positively affects your company.

One key or major decision could propel your business to the next level. It could be a partnership, a speaking gig, a specific ad campaign, an appearance or interview, etc., that does it.

But to do that, you have to keep making decisions based on the probability and potential of high returns. If you only make decisions that can only yield minor results, you'll never be able to really make a drastic improvement in your business.

## Chapter Takeaways

- Thinking about your business as an investor helps you focus on high-impact strategies and activities that produce high yields and maximum results
- Look at each aspect of your business and think in terms of "highest and best use" for your time and energy—the same goes for your team members
- Compared to traditional investing, you as a business owner have more *control* of the "engine" that produces the results

# SUMMARY

You made it to the end of this playbook! I hope this book played a vital role in laying the foundation for your marketing and business strategy and I wish you all the best in your company moving forward.

But let's recap some of the major points and takeaways…

First, we dove into the fundamentals of marketing to understand some key concepts and things to remember as you work on your strategy. We talked about being preeminent and viewing your clients as more than a transaction. We want to act and serve as their most trusted *advisors*.

We want to put their needs above our own and care for them and the goals they want to achieve. By being preeminent, you take on a different perspective, which improves how you attract, engage, and service your clients—a much more powerful and beneficial approach.

We talked about the importance of *not* being a commodity and finding ways to stand out from your market through a unique selling proposition (USP). When you find ways to differentiate, it's harder for prospects to compare you with others—especially on price.

And speaking of price, remember that people generally do *not* base their buying decisions primarily on cost for most of their life purchases. If that were the case, most people would wear the cheapest clothes, buy the cheapest food, drive the least expensive car, etc. So you never want to build your business based on being the *lowest* price. Instead, focus on the increasing the value and the benefits of what you offer.

After building a solid understanding of marketing, we then dove into where your business is today and where you want it to go. Without clear "coordinates", we can't create effective strategies for achieving your goals.

With a vision in mind for your company, we then talked about the 3 fundamental ways to grow a business and looked at various strategies you can use such as sales funnels, value ladders, a recurring revenue model, an upfront cash model, targeting specific markets based on industry and income, and the importance of following up for scaling your revenue.

In Chapter 4, we dove into the important concept of *leverage* and why as well as how to approach it for your business. The Leverage Framework breaks down numerous categories to look into for addressing your challenges and/or reaching your goals. Those categories include lessons, expertise, voices, energy, relationships, assets, growth strategies, and equipment.

We also dove into the 5 levels of *who* that make up most businesses. They include your clients, the people that make up your company, your competitors, your strategic partners, and the referrals that come from your clients. Each category plays an important role in your marketing and business growth strategy.

Chapter 5 was important—that's where we got to know your ideal client. This is the foundation of virtually *all* of your marketing efforts. By knowing your clients better than they know themselves, you're able to create more specific, meaningful messages that resonate with your target market. You'll be able to get their attention, build interest, and create desire so people who interact with your business will choose you and take action (the AIDA model). By better knowing your clients in this chapter, it also set us up for later chapters where we dove deeper into other concepts and strategies.

When trying to grow your business, it's important to study and know your competition. There's a lot you can learn from the companies with whom you're competing over the same market for. You can learn ways to improve your business from what they're doing and even *not* doing. You can create an advantage through researching client reviews. And you can study their strategy to *model* and save yourself a ton of time, energy, and money.

In Chapter 7, we dove into the 'voices' category of The Leverage Framework. This includes testimonials, social proof, endorsements, case studies, etc. When it comes to testimonials, you should build a process for requesting them into your overall strategy. You also want to guide your clients on what to say with the sample questions provided. When you do, they can touch on certain points that will better help prospects make a decision or take the next step in your business.

The Modular Marketing Method™ was a detailed process for building some of the most *important* digital marketing assets in your company. That includes your website, lead magnet, landing page, sales page, and email campaigns. This method uses a *unique* process that allows you to have a congruent message and saves you time from having to create each marketing asset independently.

The framework was designed to build your company a streamlined process for converting prospects to leads and leads into clients by utilizing the strategies from some of the world's *best* online marketers and entrepreneurs.

Once your online "ecosystem" was created, we then shifted our focus to the fourth and fifth category of who's—referrals and strategic partners. Having at least one referral marketing strategy is a *must* for any business. There's no other form of marketing that's as powerful and as cost-effective as word-of-mouth, so you have to use this to your advantage. Otherwise, you'll be missing out on tons of opportunities for growth year after year.

With strategic partners, it's all about leveraging other businesses (in a *mutually* beneficial way) to access their knowledge, skills, expertise, processes, relationships, credibility, client base, etc., to grow your business. You can do the same with other companies who want to leverage what *you* have to offer.

This is one of the most powerful ways to grow your business quickly but also for the long-term, so it's an important strategy to consider. When you have the right partners, you can find effective ways to reach your target market and effectively scale your company.

In Chapter 11, we dove into publishing content which is basically a *must* in today's digital, social media world. I shared some frameworks for your content and the importance of providing value and helping your prospects get results in advance. We also touched on the concept of using stories throughout your marketing for people at various stages in your business to increase conversions.

We then covered the affiliate marketing model to understand the benefits of *being* an affiliate and promoting *other* companies' products/services. It's a great way to supplement what you offer, and it allows you to serve clients where *your* products/services may not be able to and do so in an efficient and lucrative way.

Affiliate marketing could be just one of your revenue pillars of your Dual Parthenon Business Growth Model™. As your business grows, you can use this framework to build a structurally sound and stable business. One made up of multiple pillars to represent numerous sources of both leads and revenue, so your business is not vulnerable and underperforming like most.

We then talked about the *hidden* opportunities that lie in packaging for retail and physical goods. There are various steps you want your clients to take when they receive their orders, and you want it clear and easy for them to take those steps. This will have a huge impact on your business growth if done correctly. Most retail and ecommerce companies don't have the right strategies to maximize their product packaging and you can gain an advantage if you follow the strategies in this chapter.

And although this book isn't about operations, we covered your Achilles' Heel to find any weak or vulnerable spots in your business that could lead to its downfall. It's a topic you likely won't find in most other marketing or business books, but it's important to consider for your overall strategy. Without contingency plans for certain events that *might* occur (no matter the probability), a business can run into major trouble and implode if they don't have actions they can take immediately to minimize or eliminate the damage before it becomes too big.

The last chapter was about compounding cash flow. It was to show the importance of how a better business *today* can have a profound impact on your financial future many years from now. The Perpetual Income Model for Entrepreneurs™ is a framework that shows the flow of money from your business and how it fuels your life and your investments, which will provide you with income in both the short and long-term.

I know we covered a lot in this book, but I hope it was easy to consume and impactful for your company moving forward. Whether you're just starting your business, or you've been operating successfully for several years, I hope something in this playbook will positively change the trajectory of your company. But you have to take action with what you've learned!

## Checklist

Here's a checklist to ensure that you've implemented the most important strategies discussed throughout this book.

- My business has a clearly defined vision and goals
- My business has a simple one-liner that clearly conveys who I help and how I help them
- My business has a streamlined website and/or landing page designed for converting visitors to leads and makes it easy for people to buy
- My business has a strategic email follow-up campaign to convert leads to clients
- My business has a post-transaction email campaign to improve client success rate
- My business has a continuous follow-up strategy that provides value and maintains communication with clients over the long-term so my company can continuously make offers
- My business has core messaging pillars for publishing content and stories to share throughout my marketing

- My business has at least one referral marketing strategy that is systemized and implemented consistently
- My business has at least 3 strategic partners where I share a mutually beneficial relationship to help grow each other's businesses
- My business's product packaging (if I sell physical goods to clients) has clear steps for clients to re-order, order other products (my own or other companies'), and refer others
- My business has looked into affiliate marketing and whether it can be implemented into my business growth strategy
- My business has looked into any flaws or vulnerabilities and has plans to address them
- My business has plans to evaluate my strategies throughout the year, so my company is operating optimally

## What to Do Next

1. If you haven't already, download the free supplemental guide. It's an interactive PDF that allows you to go through each chapter's exercises so you can get the most from this book. You can save the guide to your computer and modify/update it as your business evolves. You'll also get access to *exclusive* bonuses for being a reader of this book.

**thembgplaybook.com**

2. Next, please share this book with anyone you think would find value in the strategies and concepts explained throughout. Ideally, it's an entrepreneur looking to start or grow their small company. Share it on your social media platforms with the hashtag: #thembgplaybook

3.  Please rate and review the book as it helps others decide if they should purchase it to help them with their business goals. Answer these questions in your review:

    a.  What was the problem/issue/challenge you were having before you read this book?

    b.  What did the frustration feel like as you tried to solve your problem?

    c.  What was different about this book compared to others you may have tried?

    d.  How is or will your company be better from having read this book?

4.  Read this book again (and again). Set your calendar to come back to this playbook 6 or 12 months from now. Go through some of the key strategies and exercises. Certain concepts might not "click" the first time reading it but will at later times. You might come up with new ideas or find strategies that you weren't able to the previous times you read it.

5.  If you're operating a business that generates 6 or 7-figures in *annual* revenue and would like *personalized* help with strategy or implementing what you've learned throughout this book, please visit:

**danluconsulting.com/apply**

Once more, thank you so much for reading this book and I wish you nothing but success in your business and life.

All the best,
Dan Lu